Nadja-Christina Schneider/Bettina Gräf (eds.)
Social Dynamics 2.0: Researching Change in Times
of Media Convergence

Internationale und Interkulturelle Kommunikation, Band 8
Herausgegeben von
Prof. Dr. Kai Hafez, Universität Erfurt

Nadja-Christina Schneider/Bettina Gräf (eds.)

Social Dynamics 2.0: Researching Change in Times of Media Convergence

Case studies from the Middle East and Asia

Frank & Timme

Verlag für wissenschaftliche Literatur

Umschlagabbildung: Modern Times – Telephone, electricity pole and wires,
© Angel Herrero de Frutos/iStockphoto

ISBN 978-3-86596-322-2
ISSN 1862-6106

© Frank & Timme GmbH Verlag für wissenschaftliche Literatur
Berlin 2011. Alle Rechte vorbehalten.

Das Werk einschließlich aller Teile ist urheberrechtlich geschützt.
Jede Verwertung außerhalb der engen Grenzen des Urheberrechts-
gesetzes ist ohne Zustimmung des Verlags unzulässig und strafbar.
Das gilt insbesondere für Vervielfältigungen, Übersetzungen,
Mikroverfilmungen und die Einspeicherung und Verarbeitung in
elektronischen Systemen.

Herstellung durch das atelier eilenberger, Taucha bei Leipzig.
Printed in Germany.
Gedruckt auf säurefreiem, alterungsbeständigem Papier.

www.frank-timme.de

Acknowledgements

The editors would like to express their gratitude towards the Berlin Graduate School Muslim Cultures and Societies (BGSMCS) for funding the conference in April 2010 on which this volume is based. They would also like to thank the Institute of Asian and African Studies (IAAW) at Humboldt University Berlin for supporting this conference. Finally, we would like to express our thanks to Maruan Mourad at IAAW for his assistance during the editorial process.

Contents

NADJA-CHRISTINA SCHNEIDER AND BETTINA GRÄF
Introduction 9

SARAH JURKIEWICZ
Blogging as Counterpublic? The Lebanese
and the Egyptian Blogosphere in Comparison 27

FRITZI-MARIE TITZMANN
Medialisation and Social Change – The Indian
Online Matrimonial Market as a New Field of Research 49

CLAUDIA NEF SALUZ
Dakwahkampus.com as Informal Student Web Portal
of Hizbut Tahrir Indonesia 67

CAROLA RICHTER
Media Strategies of the Major Social Movement in Egypt:
The Muslim Brothers' Website *ikhwanonline.net* 85

MARCUS MICHAELSEN
Linking Up for Change: The Internet and Social Movements in Iran 105

FREDERIK HOLST
Challenging the Notion of Neutrality – Postcolonial Perspectives
on Information- and Communication Technologies................................ 127

SASKIA SCHÄFER
Expanding the Toolbox: Discourse Analysis and Area Studies 145

List of Contributors 165

Nadja-Christina Schneider and Bettina Gräf

Introduction

1 Doing Media Research in Non-European Regions

There has been a growing interest in recent years in the increasing influence technical communication and media exert over widely different areas of society and culture in Asia and the Arab-speaking regions. A number of critical media events, such as the 9/11 attacks (as well as all subsequent terrorist attacks), the cartoon controversy, or the suppression of the "Green Movement" in Iran, and the new developments in media technology, such as the explosion in the mobile telephone market, and the launch of countless new satellite programmes and internet applications, seem to play a major role in the rapid changes these societies experience. By contrast, it is noticeable that in the disciplines of Area and Islamic Studies these new phenomena continue to be treated only to some extent, and not systematically, as an expression of far-reaching medialisation processes, which in turn possess a significant transforming potential. This is clearly inconsistent with what is expected particularly from Area and Islamic Studies, namely to provide scientifically founded explanations for complex social phenomena in non-European and/or predominantly Muslim societies, as well as to continue to improve both empirical research and theoretical approaches.

With a view to the future perspectives of Media Studies, Claus Pias recently argued that the media question – just as the gender question – is so central and productive for every discipline that "it is essential to think about new and appropriate institution forms" in order to pursue it from within the disciplines, as it "requires a lot of knowledge, which is difficult to acquire in a general course of studies like 'media'" (Pias, 2010: 40-41). In similar fashion to what is already the case with the gender perspective, Pias makes a case for bringing the media perspective more strongly into the various disciplines rather than removing it from them, as "paradoxically, one has to preserve the disciplines in order to change them" (ibid). This line of argumentation can be seamlessly incorporated into the ongoing discussion over the further development of Area and Islamic studies, at least in the German speaking region. As the dedicated efforts towards a methodical opening up demonstrate, these disciplines are already strongly differentiated beyond their rich tradition and genuine focus on 'texts', something that is particularly evident with regard to the analyses of societal contexts from a social science perspective (see for example Rudolph, 1991; Poya and Reinkowski, 2008). What is currently becoming apparent – along with the much called-for stronger linking with systematic disciplines (Johansen, 1990) – especially in the scope of the humanities' adaptation to the new B.A./M.A. courses of study, is a restructuring of Islamic Studies that points in the direction of cultural studies or historical anthropology (cf. Amman, 2003; Conermann and von Hees 2007). With regard to Area studies, Houben observes a clear tendency to no longer perceive regions as geographically and culturally fixed entities, but rather to foster a production of knowledge that shows a stronger interest in crossing borders, interconnections and exchange relations, which in turn suggests a stronger commitment towards a transregionally comparative research and transdisciplinary collaboration (Houben, 2009; Houben and Rehbein, 2010).

However, it is also important to point out that these necessary changes and reorientations within Area and Islamic Studies are not a result of departmental policy alone, but are also increasingly called for by the students themselves. On the one hand, today's students belong to a generation that has grown up in the midst of a rapid expansion of media-based communication and constant reorganization of the media and have thus developed a sound interest in as well as a distinct sense for the relevance of media-related phenomena and developments. On the other hand, the individual biographies of a growing number of students and young scholars are also an example of the new connectivities which have emerged in the course of historical and contemporary migratory movements. These connectivities offer new ways of linking regions, places, social groups, but also individuals to one another – or sometimes separating them from one another –, and this makes the perspectives of these students and junior researchers particularly relevant to our discussion context (cf. on connectivity Hepp and Krotz and Moores and Winter, 2006; Tomlinson, 2002).

And finally, the enormous public, that is non-academic interest in new media and technical communication should also be acknowledged as a decisive factor that has prepared the ground for an increasing awareness and serious consideration of media developments in non-European contexts within Area and Islamic Studies. Along with the previously mentioned critical media events, this encompasses in particular the role and function of social media (Facebook, Friendster, etc.) in social and political movements, as well as the worldwide phenomenon of citizen journalism and the global success of non-Western film industries such as Bollywood or Nollywood, and not least the increasing medialisation of religion and faith. The above are just a few examples of topics of major interest not only to the media makers but also to their public. It is no coincidence that, especially in association with the currently controversial issues "criticism of Islam" and "Islamophobia", the question about who the experts for these new phenomena are and where they can be found may remind us of Edward Said's work "Covering Islam: How the media and the experts determine how we see the rest of the world" (Said, 1997), because when the "Islam" issue became a media event during the late 1970s as a result of the political upheavals in Iran and Pakistan, the "critical absence", in Said's words, of academic experts led to the establishment of an authority composed in part of self-appointed experts on Islam, something that is also clearly perceptible today. In Said's view, historians and Islamic studies scholars failed to recognize the necessity of immediately becoming involved in this dangerous media discussion and global diffusion of media-produced images of Islam, thus totally underestimating the effects of these media images. This has changed fundamentally in the meantime, as, particularly within Islamic Studies, systematic-empirical research relating to the media representation of Islam, especially with regard to stereotyping and constructing an enemy concept, has become one of the most crucial media-related issues (cf. for example Hafez, 2010 and 2002; Spielhaus, 2010; Schiffer, 2010 and 2005; Amir-Moazami, 2007).

Yet even though the situation today is fundamentally different, with academics being aware of how much they rely on the media especially when researching media-related phenomena, we consider it very important – not least in view of the threat of persisting but also new essentialising terms such as „cyber jihad", „cyber Islam", or „iMuslims" – that disciplines like Area and Islamic Studies pay more attention to distributing knowledge and competences pertaining to phenomena of medialisation not only in research but also in academic teaching (see in this respect Wilke, 2002).

The following assumptions have given rise to three key considerations in this edited volume:

I. A stronger and more systematic commitment towards in-depth research on medialisation with respect to non-European and/or predominantly Muslim societies is necessary if we want to attain the level of density which has long been standard in media-related research on Europe and North America.
II. Advanced knowledge of the respective region, including regional language skills, is an important prerequisite when researching the distribution, appropriation and effects of the media in Asian and Arab societies, also in order to avoid a mere transference of concepts based on the specific historical conditions and developments in Europe and North America (cf. Curran and Park, 2000; Thussu, 2009).
III. The conceptualisation of both existing and new research projects should take into account more clearly than in the past the reflexive relationship between media technologies – including their formative context – and the manner in which these media are appropriated and used in local contexts.

2   Focussing on Internet-based Communication

Since the dawn period of the internet as we know it in the early 1990s, the world's largest computer network of public and private users has been the subject of many promising and visionary ideas. Through the fast, uncomplicated and distance-eliminating communication opportunities, people would be able to experience a direct and decentralised communication culture, emancipated from any forms of hierarchy. There was talk of more democracy, interactivity and immediacy (Amerika, 1996: 262). However, doubts were raised too, particularly in view of the unequal distribution on a regional as well as on a strata-specific level (Wurzbacher, 2000). Today, over one billion people use the internet. The doubts remain, but the developments go on. With the beginning of the 21st century came Web 2.0, also known as social media or social networks. These expressions identify a new generation of internet technologies allowing users to create content themselves, with the term *prosumer* describing this new mixture of producer and consumer of information (cf. Kösch, 2007, see also the term *produsage*, Burns, 2008). Some examples of these new applications are wikis, blogs and chat rooms, as well as social networks such as Facebook and MySpace, which enable users to create so-called user profiles and upload photographs and videos. Also, commercial service portals such as Flickr allow users to upload photographs on a website and make them available for others to view. Wikis are a good example for illustrating the novelty of these applications. Whereas communication, including such on the internet, formerly consisted of one writer and one reader and was still regarded as mass communication since it constituted a one-sided but public transmission of a message to many others (Baumann and Schwender 2000), many people today can contribute to a common text – the so-called hypertext. Accordingly, users can not only read information, but are also able to change it, comment on it or even delete it in principle, though certain rules apply to the latter (cf. Amerika, 1996; Kösch, 2007). An old dream that Bertolt Brecht had envisaged in his theory of the radio finally seems to come true (cf. Wurzbacher, 2000).

Yet what type of change are we really dealing with? Are the traditional structures of communication between author and the public shifting? Has our communication in and through the net become more emancipated? Which topics are of interest to most people, and are the old promises kept? What contents concern users regarding the region they live in, the political and social problems they are confronted with, and the political structures they are involved in? So far, research on phenomena associated with the electronic media and non-European regions has been unsystematic and fragmentary. Albrecht Hofheinz has subdivided the research work on the Arabic-language internet into two groups, the separating line being the critical event of September 11, 2001: Before 9/11, a major part of this literature dealt with new politics and emerging public spheres in the 1990s, and from 2001 onwards, "terrorist activities" and the media as battlefield emerged as the new focal areas of internet-related research (Hofheinz, 2004).

Besides focussing on political events and major political topics, one needs to address the particularities of the use of digital media in non-European languages while also taking into consideration the imbrications and cross-linking within the global media environment in terms of the content published as well as of the technology, the financing and the players involved. A regional allocation of certain players, for example, is not so simple to undertake due to the fact that Saudi investors co-finance the American satellite television market, and also because most companies and private persons in the Middle East make use of American internet services, such as Google, Facebook, YouTube, BlogSpot or Amazon (see for example Sakr, 2005; Khater, 2010). But then again, we observe specific local or national processes of change in connection with gender relations (see for example Wheeler, 2004), relationships between generations (see for example Braune, 2008), and relations of religious authority (cf. Khamis, 2010; Sakr, 2007), brought about through the active use of the media.

An "Islamic internet"?

In addition, some research work deals with the so-called Islamic internet and with websites pursuing an Islamic agenda. Though they only constitute a small part of the internet-based communication in and from Asia and the Arab-speaking world[1], these sites are a phenomenon that has been booming during the last ten years and remains very popular both with journalists and with students. The history of those sites is explained by Jon Anderson und Yves Gonzales-Quijano (2004) in three stages: at first, it was Muslim students of science or technical subjects at Western universities, who began to use the internet during the 1980s. Here they found more like-minded people who were also searching for answers as to how to apply Islamic rules on everyday life. These discussions were characterised by the absence of contributions from *'ulama* (Islamic legal scholars). The first IT companies specialising in Arab-language software (for example *Sakhr*, which was established in Kuwait in 1982) came into being during the same period. During the second phase in the 1990s the internet gained popularity, and official institutions, be they governments, political parties, social and political movements, or educational institutions, started producing websites with Islamic content. Those sites were no different to the representations of the respective institutions outside the internet in terms of their content („they preserved their formats and dictions

---

1   8% religious, i.e. Islamic, websites were among the 100 most-visited sites on the Arabic-language web in November 2003. (cf. Hofheinz: „Das Internet", 2004: 460).

of formal, official pronouncements", id., 63). The third phase saw the expansion of the Arabic language on the internet thanks to the Internet Explorer 5.0 by Microsoft. More and more programmers and producers of content became involved, which led to a diversification of the Islamic internet. New technological accomplishments, such as interactive modules or the ability to upload and save large amounts of data, further contributed to the development of the dynamic Islamic internet we find today: „It is multi-dimensional, user-oriented, modulated to the settings and concerns of professionals, and set within the concerns of pious middle classes" (id., 65).

Websites with representative functions continue to exist, yet the number of religion-related projects run by individuals or groups in the shape of portals, blogs, and videoblogs is continuously rising in today's Web 2.0. As of 2007, for example, we find Islamic adaptations of the video portal *YouTube.com*, named *IslamTube.com* and *FaithTube.com*. With a few exceptions (see, for instance, Bunt 2009 and Richter, 2010), these latest developments have not yet been critically incorporated in scientific publications, but are reflected on in the form of journalistic articles. Research on the developments described as phase three of the Islamic internet by Anderson and Gonzales-Quijano has so far concentrated largely on fatwas (Islamic legal opinions), which is no surprise inasmuch as fatwas are an interactively oriented genre of Islamic law (see Bunt, 2000 and 2003; Brückner, 2001). The study of media fatwas can help to fulfill a desideratum in the research of the internet in non-European societies, namely to take up and process knowledge traditions and concepts of the regions over which we concern ourselves in association with media and communication related research (cf. Gräf, 2010).

However, the question that needs to be asked is how fortunate the choice of the description „Islamic internet" is, as it implies that all users are Muslims who communicate exclusively with other Muslims and discuss solely Islam-related subjects. The above assumptions are inadequate essentialisations. Yet we must ask ourselves how specific religious, political, and cultural phenomena of internet-based communication can be researched without the need to be labelled as, for example, "Christian", "leftist", or "pop culture" internet.

3 Diversity, Dynamics and Contextualisation of Internet-based Communication

In many respects, the contributions to this edited volume demonstrate new perspectives and lines of thought. First of all, communication over the internet has manifold formats and platforms, which is reflected in the various articles within this volume. The media practises of bloggers are examined, as is the importance of websites and web portals to political movements. The authors are concerned not only with the content produced, which is often politically alternative, but primarily with the ways different players handle this content both offline and within social networks like Facebook. The diversity of internet-based communication forms is illustrated not only by means of political issues, but also through the analysis of new social practises, such as the search for a life partner in matrimonial websites.

Yet the authors do not focus exclusively on the one medium, the internet; they also examine the interaction between different forms of media and the associated processes. SARAH YURKIEWICZ in her contribution about the Egyptian and Lebanese blogospheres demonstrates how blogs commenting on news and articles which originate from so-called traditional media and, reversely, the references to blogs in the established press bring about a convergence of communications produced online and in the press, which makes hitherto marginalised opinions accessible to a wider readership. At the same time she refers to the issue based and temporary character of activities of many bloggers as a new form of political and social action. In YURKIEWICZ's article, the content analysis of blogs goes hand in hand with the question about the reasons behind people's commitment to public writing in the form of blogs. Often it is one's personal interests and professional career that play a significant role, as the author identifies in her article about individual bloggers, thus putting into perspective an important concern of this volume, namely the contextualisation of internet-based communication (see also Silver, 2000).

A further aspect is her dealing with counterpublics (as defined by Nancy Fraser, 1992), a concept normatively charged with the history of European and American societies. She delves into the question how this type of political counternarrative and alternative presentation of news by means of blogs can be conceptualised in academic work, even (or especially) when the societies described are not liberal-democratic systems. CLAUDIA NEF in her article about the Indonesian internet portal *Dakwahkampus.com* touches on a similar point. She challenges the dichotomy between deliberative and disciplining effects of media-based communication, which she deems too simple in the analyses existing to date, and suggests a more flexible view of the media-based procelytisation practises of *Hizb ut Tahrir* members, which always entail both indoctrination and discussions. Furthermore, NEF calls into question the rigid demarcation between members and non-members of *Hizb ut Tahrir* and gives greater weight to the specific dynamics and structures of groups of "fans" and "sympathizers" (online as well as offline) as well as to the limits to be negotiated between public and private action. She thereby stresses the need for a new sensitivity for the specific dynamics and vitality of public communication and political action in times of social media and convergence.

Another author who looks into the dynamics set off through internet-based communication in her article is CAROLA RICHTER. With the aid of specific communication strategies used by Egypt's Muslim Brothers, she illustrates the extent to which the success of social and political movements is determined by their respective communication skills. Especially with the strategic use of the website *Ikhwanonline.com* in current political debates in Egypt, the Muslim Brothers and their agenda seem to reach a wider public than before. Yet RICHTER does not focus exclusively on *Ikhwanonline.com* in her article. The website serves as a case study to illustrate the importance of the so-called alternative media for the study of social movements in authoritarian regimes.

An aspect that has not been sufficiently looked at in connection with the study of internet-based communication is the issue of the "T" in ICT (Information and Communication Technologies), which FREDERIK HOLST discusses in his article, turning avowedly against a view which either totally ignores the impact of technology-inherent meanings, power structures and ideologies on post-colonial societies, or simply denies it in the assumption that technology is fundamentally "neutral". In addition to the prevailing perception of ICT as providers of growth, development and liberal values – or, depending on the perspective adopted, as "overrated" media technologies in this respect – HOLST also makes a case for adopting a firmly postcolonial perspective in a regionally embedded media research – a perspective which should be application oriented at least in the sense that it seeks ways to promote participation both in and through ICT in postcolonial societies.

4 Studying Processes of Medialisation and Social Change

The terms medialisation and mediatization[2] have become key terms of a new orientation in the disciplines of media and communication studies. Instead of concentrating on the "effects" or the impact of the media, as has been the dominating concept for a long time, emphasis is now increasingly being placed on processes of social change, within which technical communication media are ascribed a central role (Krotz, 2003 and 2007). The two terms are used sometimes almost synonymously, but also often with differentiated meanings which result from the diverging positions of what is observed as the actual subject of media and communication sciences, the conceptual understanding of media they are based on, and consequently which media are actually included in the discussion (Krotz and Stöber, 2008; Meyen, 2009).

In terms of an independent media perspective within the scope of Area and Islamic Studies, adopting one or both of the terms "medialisation" and "mediatisation" as an approach is undoubtedly not without its problems, since they are subject to an ongoing inner-disciplinary discussion within Media and Communication studies. How the outcome of this discussion can be associated with our context here has to be identified by means of concrete research projects and theory oriented discussions. Yet the potential of an epistemological framework based on a medialisation approach appears to be great already, also for non-European regions and/or predominantly Muslim societal contexts. For a start, on a very fundamental level, it provides the opportunity for the introduction of a media perspective that does not concentrate exclusively on the changes in communication technology over the last 20 or 30 years, but also takes into account the specific historical prerequisites and the local socio-cultural, political and economic underlying circumstances when observing

---

2   In the sense of a comprehensive meta-process, Krotz and Hepp in the German-speaking world (and increasingly also in the Anglophone domain) have coined the analytical term "mediatization" to describe the process of the increasing penetration of media, a process that refers to the global proliferation of technology-based communication media across the various social and cultural fields in a historical long-term perspective (cf. Hartmann & Hepp, 2010; Krotz, 2007).

contemporary and present-day developments. This historical perspective seems indispensable in order to make valid statements about temporary or permanent processes which are to be studied within an accepted dialectic of developments in the media and of social change.

In our view, social change never originates exclusively from the media or from technical innovations; rather, it depends largely on the conceptions with which people adopt media technologies, on the media practises they develop, and on how they integrate these in their everyday life (cf. Giesecke, 1991). In her concluding comment at the conference, Dorothea Schulz made a case for a regionally embedded media research as well as for the study of media-related processes instead of the media themselves, as the varying types of sociability and communication practises greatly influence how media are used (cf. Schulz, 2007). At the same time attention must be given to the respective economic, legal and political structures, as well as to the type of social processes that preceded the change of habits in communication and thus enabled these in the first place.

The article by MARCUS MICHAELSEN in this volume illustrates this quite exemplarily. Here, aside from looking into the role of the internet in social movements in Iran, the author also analyses the reciprocal influence between the internet and social movements. He, too, observes that a media-centric perspective, though it may contribute to the notion of a "Twitter revolution", or to the pessimistic estimation that the revolution "will not be tweeted after all", will miss the most important point in both cases if the observation primarily focuses on communication technology and not on the people and contexts within which this technology becomes relevant. On the basis of his empirical research in Iran, however, MICHAELSEN comes to the conclusion that the internet could indeed be beneficial to the vital and committed political and social movements in the country, and that in some cases it already is, especially with view to the women's rights movement as well as to reform-oriented players. Social networks on the internet open up new opportunities for communitisation, information, and mobilisation, not least for Iranian journalists and publishers affected by the state's rigid censorship of the press and control of the media, especially since 2005. In MICHAELSEN's view, however, the online media can in no way be considered a substitute for a free press or for other forms of media with a significantly larger scope, such as television or radio. We think that his article also suggests the possibility of a future research perspective focussing more on the media environment in Iran and on intermedial practices and connectivities, instead of giving priority to individual media, as was the case with audio tapes during the Iranian Revolution or the internet in the context of the Green Movement. One question that could be posed is whether the practises of its users in Iran could make the internet a true *intermedium* that spans bridges to other types of media and facilitates the establishment of new media forms, which could radically reconfigure the Iranian media environment and thus lead to a lasting transformation of the communicative order.

Naturally, medialisation processes and social change occur at different speeds and with varying degrees of transformational power around the world. However, the quasi-teleological explanation attempts that have been dominant for a long time are rather problematic in our view, as they always carry the risk of an unreflective reproduction of binary categories and culturalist approaches of modernisation and development theories (cf. Meyen, 2009). A functionalist view on the media that regards them either as bringers of "modernisation" and "development", as was predominantly and unquestioningly common for a long time with regard to postcolonial societies in Asia and Africa, or sweepingly blames them for the "cultural uprootedness", "westernisation", and the growing consumerism of the younger generations, as is the case with some critical discourses on media, is today rightfully criticized as being too restricted.

We therefore understand the approach through the term "medialisation" as open-ended, for it should not determine which direction global media developments and their associated changes in communication practises will pursue. On the one hand it is quite possible that an accelerated medialisation and the transnational and transcultural dynamics of media developments, which Hepp describes as "moulding forces of the media", could lead to an increased "individualisation", "deterritorialisation" and "immediacy" (cf. Hepp and Hjarvard and Lundby, 2010; Hartmann and Hepp, 2010). Yet this is by no means a definite or unequivocal development, for processes of medialisation can at the same time also promote totally contrasting tendencies. Though seemingly contradictory, tendencies that go both ways are closely interlinked and can be observed distinctly in the example of the rapidly expanding online Indian matrimonial market, which FRITZI-MARIE TITZMANN in her article presents as a new area of research particularly relevant for studying the connection between medialisation and socio-cultural change. On the one hand her article looks at changes in the perception of concepts like love, family, and marriage among India's young generation. On the other hand she demonstrates – with regard to the various links of matrimonial websites to other communication media and non-internet practises – how the claimed reflexive influence of media technologies and acquired media skills becomes concrete in a way that one could describe as practised intermediality or transmediality. With respect to these new media configurations and practises, there is again one medium that plays a key role, a medium considered by many to belong to a past era: the press.

Coming to discuss the medium of the press in the conclusion of an edited volume that predominantly presents case studies focusing on internet-based communication may seem somewhat paradoxical or even anachronistic at first glance. However, in Asia and the Arab-speaking world, the so-called conventional media (newspapers, radio, and television) have not been superseded by the "new" medium that is the internet, or become obsolete in the sense that they've all had their respective heyday and then fallen into oblivion (see in this respect the pointed criticism by Rajagopal, 2009). On the contrary, particularly – but not exclusively – in countries like India and China we have seen during the last two decades an unprecedented upsurge of print media going hand in hand with the concurrent boom of television, radio, and also the internet (see in this respect Schneider, 2005: 15-54). And yet the focus and interest of Asia-related academic research still lie on the study of individual media, currently clearly privileging digital and audiovisual media, while research on print media is considered antiquated to a greater or lesser extent.

The question which theoretical and methodological approaches Area and Islamic Studies could and should adopt in future becomes more complex due to the specific history and media developments in Asian countries as well as in the Arab-speaking world. The discussion regarding the necessary modifications of existing theoretical models and terms that were mostly developed on the basis of historical experiences and empirical data from Europe and North America is still in its early stages and will certainly continue over the next few years. And it also remains to be seen if any new theoretical approaches can be worked out on the basis of the regional contexts examined in this volume, which may even be of interest to a discussion on media theory with regard to "Western" societies. As researchers, we must of course include ourselves in this critical reflection and become involved in the discourses we examine, acknowledge, and reveal, as SASKIA LOUISE SCHÄFER describes in her article. Precisely because discourse analysis offers the opportunity to link media-related discourses to discourses in other areas of society, and thus to avoid the dangers of excessive mediacentrism and insufficient contextualisation of mediated communication, she sees great potential in the linking of discourse-analytical approaches and regionally embedded research on media and medialisation.

We hope that the present volume can contribute to the discussion as to what the features of an independent and systematic media perspective in the disciplinary framework of Area and Islamic Studies should be, and to what form a transdisciplinary dialogue with regard to a regionally embedded research on media and medialisation could take.

Bibliography

AMERIKA, M., 1996. Avant-Pop und die neuen elektronischen Medien. In: M. KLEPPER & R. MAYER & E.P. SCHNECK, ed. *Hyper-Kultur: Zur Fiktion des Computerzeitalters.* Berlin, New York: Walter de Gruyter, pp. 253-268.

AMIR-MOAZAMI, S., 2007. *Politisierte Religion: Der Kopftuchstreit in Deutschland und Frankreich.* Bielefeld: transcript.

AMMAN, L. 2003. Islamwissenschaften. In: K. E. MÜLLER, ed. *Phänomen Kultur: Perspektiven und Aufgaben der Kulturwissenschaften.* Bielefeld: transcript, p. 82.

ANDERSON, J. W. & GONZALEZ-QUIJANO, Y., 2004. Technological Mediation and the Emergence of Transnational Publics. In: A. SALVATORE & D. EICKELMAN, ed. *Public Islam and the Common Good,* Leiden: Brill, pp. 53-74.

APPADURAI, A. & BRECKENRIDGE, C. A., 1988. Editors' Comment. *Public Culture,* 1 (1).

BAUMANN, H. & SCHWENDER, C., ED., 2000. *Kursbuch Neue Medien 2000: Ein Reality-Check.* Stuttgart, München: DVA.

BRAUNE, INES, 2008. *Aneignungen des Globalen. Internet-Alltag in der arabischen Welt. Eine Fallstudie in Marokko.* Bielefeld: transcript.

BRÜCKNER, M., 2001. *Fatwas zum Alkohol unter dem Einfluss neuer Medien im 20. Jahrhundert.* Arbeitsmaterialien zum Orient, Band 7. Würzburg: Ergon.

BUNT, G. R., 2000. *Virtually Islamic: Computer-mediated Communication and Cyber Islamic Environments.* Cardiff: University of Wales Press.

BUNT, G. R., 2003. *Islam in the Digital Age: E-Jihad, Online Fatwas and Cyber Islamic Environments.* London: Pluto Press.

BUNT, G. R., 2009. *iMuslims: Rewiring the House of Islam.* Chapel Hill, NC: University of North Carolina Press & London: Hurst & Co.

BURNS, A., 2008. *Blogs, Wikipedia, Second Life, and Beyond: From Production to Produsage.* New York: Peter Lang.

CONERMANN, S. & VON HEES, S., ed., 2007. *Islamwissenschaft als Kulturwissenschaft I – Historische Anthropologie/Mentalitätsgeschichte: Ansätze und Möglichkeiten.* Schenefeld/Hamburg: EB-Verlag.

CURRAN, J. & PARK, M.-J., ed., 2000. *De-Westernizing Media Studies.* London (u.a.): Routledge.

FRASER, N., 1992. Rethinking the Public Sphere: A Contribution to the Critique of Actually Existing Democracy. In: C. CALHOUN, ed. *Habermas and the Public Sphere.* Cambridge a.o.: MIT Press, pp. 109-142.

GIESECKE, M., 1991. *Der Buchdruck in der frühen Neuzeit – Eine historische Fallstudie über die Durchsetzung neuer Informations- und Kommunikationstechnologien.* Frankfurt/M.: Suhrkamp.

GRÄF, B., 2010. *Medien-Fatwas@Yusuf al-Qaradawi: Die Popularisierung des islamischen Rechts.* ZMO-Studien 27. Berlin: Klaus Schwarz Verlag.

HAFEZ, K., 2002. *Die politische Dimension der Auslandsberichterstattung. Bd. 2: Das Nahost- und Islambild in der deutschen überregionalen Presse.* Baden-Baden: Nomos.

HAFEZ, K., 2010. Mediengesellschaft – Wissensgesellschaft? Gesellschaftliche Entstehungsbedingungen der Islambilder deutscher Medien. In: T. G. SCHNEIDERS, ed. *Islamfeindlichkeit, wenn die Grenzen der Kritik verschwimmen*. Wiesbaden: VS Verlag für Sozialwissenschaften, pp. 101-118.

HARTMANN, M. & HEPP, A., ed., 2010. *Die Mediatisierung der Alltagswelt*. Wiesbaden: VS Verlag für Sozialwissenschaften.

HEPP, A. & HJARVARD, S. & LUNDBY, K., ed., 2010. Mediatization – Empirical perspectives: An Introduction to a Special Issue, *Communications*, 35 (3), pp. 223-228.

HEPP, A. & MOORES, S. & WINTER, C. & KROTZ, F., eds. 2006. *Konnektivität, Netzwerk und Fluss*. Wiesbaden: VS Verlag für Sozialwissenschaften.

HOFHEINZ, A., 2004. Das Internet und sein Beitrag zum Wertewandel in arabischen Gesellschaften. In: S. Faath, ed. *Politische und gesellschaftliche Debatten in Nordafrika, Nah- und Mittelost. Inhalte, Träger, Perspektiven*. Hamburg: Deutsches Orient-Institut, pp. 449-472.

HOUBEN, V., 2009. Neuaufstellung der Regionalstudien, *Asien*, 111 (Editorial), pp. 7-9.

HOUBEN, V. & REHBEIN, B., 2010. Regional- und Sozialwissenschaften nach dem Aufstieg des globalen Südens, *Asien*, 116, pp. 149-156.

JOHANSEN, B., 1990. Politics and Scholarship: The Development of Islamic Studies in the Federal Republic of Germany. In: T. Y. ISMAEL, ed. *Middle East Studies. International Perspectives on the State of the Art*. New York: Praeger, pp. 71-130.

KHAMIS, S., 2010. New Media and Social Change in Rural Egypt, *Arab Media and Society*, 11, [online] Available at: http://www.arabmediasociety.com/?article=758.

KHATER, R., 2010. Digital Protectionism: Preparing for the Coming Internet Embargo, *Arab Media and Society*, 11, [online] Available at: http://www.arabmediasociety.com/?article=766.

KÖSCH, S., 2007. Digital Consumer Culture: Is It What We Think It Is?, (Paper at the conference: *Muslim Digital Consumer Culture*, Goethe-Institut, November 2007).

KROTZ, F., 2003. Zivilisationsprozess und Mediatisierung: Zum Zusammenhang von Medien- und Gesellschaftswandel. In: M. BEHMER & F. KROTZ & R. STÖBER & C. WINTER, ed. *Medienentwicklung und gesellschaftlicher Wandel*. Wiesbaden: Westdeutscher Verlag, pp. 15-38.

KROTZ, F., 2007. *Mediatisierung: Fallstudien zum Wandel von Kommunikation*. Wiesbaden: VS Verlag.

KROTZ, F. & STÖBER, R., 2008. Ein Fall von sprachlicher Prägnanz? Überlegungen zu „Mediatisierung" und „Medialisierung", *aviso*, 47 (October), pp. 13-14.

MEYEN, M., 2009. Medialisierung. In: HANS-BREDOW-INSTITUT, ed. *Medien & Kommunikationswissenschaft*, 57. Jahrgang, Heft 1, Hamburg, pp. 23-38.

PIAS, C., 2010. „Was mit Medien…". Ist Medienreflexion institutionalisierbar? Interview: Jürgen Kaube. In: WISSENSCHAFTSKOLLEG ZU BERLIN, ed. *Köpfe und Ideen 2010*. pp. 36-41.

POYA, A. & REINKOWSKI, M., ed., 2008. *Das Unbehagen in der Islamwissenschaft: Ein klassisches Fach im Scheinwerferlicht der Politik und der Medien*. Bielefeld: transcript.

Rajagopal, A., 2009. *The Indian Public Sphere: Readings in Media History*. New Delhi a.o.: OUP India.

Richter, C., 2010. Virtual Mobilisation: The Internet and Political Activism in Egypt. *Orient-German Journal of Politics, Economics and Culture of the Middle East. Focus: The Muslim World and the Internet*, 51(1), pp. 16-24.

Rudolph, E., 1991. *Westliche Islamwissenschaft im Spiegel muslimischer Kritik: Grundzüge und aktuelle Merkmale einer innerislamischen Diskussion*. Berlin: Klaus Schwarz.

Said, Edward W., 1997. *Covering Islam. How the Media and Experts Determine how we See the Rest of the World*. London a.o.: Vintage.

Sakr, N., 2005. Channels of Interaction: The Role of Gulf-Owned Media Firms in Globalisation. In: P. Dresch & J. Piscatori, ed. *Monarchies and Nations: Globalisation and Identity in the Arab States of the Gulf*. London a.o.: Tauris, pp. 34-51.

Sakr, N., ed., 2007. *Arab Media and Political Renewal. Community, Legitimacy and Public Life*. London, N.Y.: I.B. Tauris.

Schiffer, S., 2005. *Die Darstellung des Islams in der Presse: Sprache, Bilder, Suggestionen; eine Auswahl von Techniken und Beispielen*. Würzburg: Ergon.

Schiffer, S., 2010. Grenzenloser Hass im Internet: Wie „islamkritische" Aktivisten in Weblogs argumentierten. In: T. G. Schneiders, ed. *Islamfeindlichkeit, wenn die Grenzen der Kritik verschwimmen*. Wiesbaden: VS Verlag für Sozialwissenschaften, pp. 341-362.

Schneider, N.-C., 2005. *Zur Darstellung von 'Kultur' und 'kultureller Differenz' im indischen Mediensystem: Die indische Presse und die Repräsentation des Islams im Rahmen der Zivilrechtsdebatte, 1985-87 und 2003*. Berlin: Logos.

Schulz, D., 2007. Evoking Moral Community, Fragmenting Muslim Discourse: Sermon Audio-recordings and the Reconfiguration of Public Debate in Mali, *Journal of Islamic Studies*, 26, pp. 39-71.

Silver, D., 2000. Locking Backwards, Looking Forwards: Cyberculture Studies 1990-2000. In: D. Gauntlett, ed. *Web.Studies: Rewiring Media Studies for the Digital Age*. London, N.Y.: Arnold, pp. 19-30.

Spielhaus, R., 2010. Media Making Muslims: the Construction of a Muslim Community in Germany through Media Debate, *Contemporary Islam* 4: 11-27.

Thussu, D. K., ed., 2009. *Internationalizing Media Studies*. New York u.a.: Routledge.

Tomlinson, J., 2002. Internationalismus, Globalisierung und kultureller Imperialismus. In: A. Hepp & M. Löffelholz, ed. *Grundlagentexte zur transkulturellen Kommunikation*. Konstanz: UVK, pp. 140-163.

Wheeler, D. L., 2004. Blessings and Curses: Women and the Internet Revolution in the Arab World. In: S. Naomi, ed. *Women and Media in the Middle East. Power Through Self-Expression*. London, N.Y: I.B. Tauris, pp. 138-161,

Wheeler, D. L., 2006. *The Internet in the Middle East. Global Expectations and Local Imaginations in Kuwait*, Albany: State University of New York Press.

WILKE, J., 2002. Internationale Kommunikationsforschung: Entwicklungen, Forschungsfelder, Perspektiven. In: K. HAFEZ, ed. *Die Zukunft der internationalen Kommunikationswissenschaft in Deutschland*. Hamburg: Deutsches Übersee-Institut, pp. 13-38.

WURZBACHER, RALF, 2000. Chomsky revisited. In: H. BAUMANN & C. SCHWENDER, eds.: *Kursbuch Neue Medien 2000. Ein Reality-Check*. Stuttgart/München: DVA, pp. 367-386.

All URLs checked for availability and content (14 Feb 2011).

Sarah Jurkiewicz

Blogging as Counterpublic?
The Lebanese and the Egyptian Blogosphere in Comparison

Especially in research on media in the Middle East, blogging "has been hailed as a new opportunity for public communication, political activism, and a democratic public sphere" (Anderson, 2009). According to Walter Armbrust, the focus on the political effects of new media even seems to be a "new obsession" within Middle Eastern Studies (Armbrust, 2007: 532). Nevertheless there is a lack of valuable concepts to describe the phenomena of blogging and internet-based communication in the region.[1] Which concepts could be transferred or extended in order to grasp the dynamics of blogging and its relation to the wider public sphere in the Middle East?[2] Marc Lynch (2007a: 5) suggests that even "(i)f blogs cannot constitute a genuine public sphere without reaching a mass audience, they still might form a counter-public, an incubator of new ideas and new identities which evolves alongside and slowly reshapes the mainstream public form below". Indeed, it is tempting to understand blogging as a counterpublic, especially under restricted political conditions, because it often provides different or "alternative" information and "counters" representations, both those of governments as well as representation of the media. However the notion of a "counterpublic"– like its counterpart the public sphere – is itself normative and ambiguous (Wimmer, 2007) and in need of revision. First, prominent formulations of the concepts, like those of Nancy Fraser (1992), do not take into account new communications technology. Second, these notions emanate from a "democratic public sphere", which raises the question whether they can be transferred to other forms of publics.

The aim of this article is therefore twofold: one is to adapt the concept of "counterpublics" to the phenomena of blogging and two is to transfer it to

---

1 Following Markam and Baym, I do not spell internet with a capital "I", because that suggests that the internet is a place or a being and gives it a rather problematic agency (Markham and Baym, 2009: 7).
2 For general discussions about internet/blogging and the public sphere, see Dahlgren (2005) and Ó Baoill (2004).

concrete contexts in the Middle East. Two distinct blogospheres that have attracted attention during the last year are the empirical basis for this discussion: First, the Lebanese blogosphere, which has been internationally recognized through its reporting during the Independence Intifada of 2005 and the July War of 2006 and is especially active in "times of crisis"; and second, the Egyptian blogosphere, which is the largest Arabic blogosphere[3], has become "a blueprint for online activists in the Arab world" (Radsch, 2008: 11) and is known for being one of the most politically active blogospheres. These two cases reveal specificities of blogospheres and distinct cultures of (counter)publics.

Whereas my findings on the Lebanese blogospheres are grounded in fieldwork among Lebanese bloggers in Beirut during winter 2009/2010, for the presentation on the Egyptian blogosphere I rely on other researchers' documentation as well as talks with some key figures of the Egyptian blogosphere that I had during the *Second Arab Bloggers Meeting* in Beirut in December 2009.

1 The Lebanese and Egyptian Blogosphere: Development and Groups

Before turning to the blogospheres, a short note on the phrase "national blogosphere" needs to be made. Initially, the term blogosphere designated all the blogging activities worldwide, but meanwhile it is also been used to describe specific national clusters of blogging. A recent study on the Arabic blogosphere confirms that blogging is mainly nationally framed, since most of the interlinking is with bloggers from the same country (Etling et al., 2009).[4] Also, the self-representation of bloggers in a national blog aggregator, i.e., a website in which blogs from or about a certain country are assembled[5], justifies us in speaking of blogospheres of specific countries. Nevertheless, the term involves the danger of overlooking the internal boundaries (Klaus, 2009: 253). Bloggers from one country don't link up to just anybody, but rather mostly to

---

[3] Egypt has both the largest population and the largest online population in the Arab world (Etling et al., 2009).
[4] The report by the *The Berkman Centre for Internet & Society* is a quantitative study of the blogosphere based on a large social network analysis.
[5] See http://lebanonaggregator.blogspot.com/ and for Egypt: http://www.omraneya.net/.

bloggers who are in one sense or another close, may it be politically or personally. Blogging is thus, as Jon Anderson puts it, "user-distributed, like social networking sites" (Anderson, 2009). These objections kept in mind, the notion still remains useful as a working tool.

A) The Lebanese Blogosphere [6]

The Lebanese blogosphere has increased enormously after former Lebanese Prime Minister Hariri's assassination in 2005 and the following demonstrations for the independence from Syria, the so-called Cedar Revolution or Independence Intifada. Between February and June 2005 alone, several hundred blogs were created (Haugbolle, 2007) in which a wide range of issues, mainly related to the current political situation, were discussed.

The blogosphere then experienced a second peak in the July War of 2006, during which another hundred new blogs were launched. During the war it offered alternative news to press and TV coverage. Bloggers wrote pieces of war journalism and personal descriptions of life under siege. After the end of the war, several blogs stopped, others were continued only in times of conflict.[7] The activity of the blogosphere as a whole can therefore be described as irregular, and it is strongly linked to political circumstances. Nevertheless, new blogs covering a wide range of thematic fields were launched since 2007.

The thematic focus of the Lebanese blogosphere has been domestic politics and all issues related to Palestine. While blogs that provide political commentary and links to newspaper articles were dominant in the beginning, after 2006, when the political situation was rather stable, the focus has broadened. Bloggers comment on social issues, mock political discussions, post about cultural events in Beirut, and write rather personal stories of daily life, but also engage in political activism. They thereby mix several genres and styles; political commentary can be followed by a posted poem or a personal story. This makes it rather difficult to maintain the division between political blogs and personal blogs. However, one could say there are classical journalistic

---

6   The overview does not include the publishing platform *maktoob*, because these bloggers are according to my observation not among the A-list bloggers. Furthermore they are absent from the Lebanese blog aggregator as well as blogger-meetings in Beirut. This issue deserves more detailed study that I will follow up in my next fieldwork.

7   For example *Funky Zarathustra* (http://funkyzarathustra.blogspot.com/), who notes that she is "blogging mostly during conflicts ie. every four months or so".

blogs and strictly personal blogs. Furthermore, at the beginning of 2010, a new association of Lebanese bloggers, the *lebloggers*[8] was established, which covered the municipal elections in spring 2010 and envisages spreading the culture of blogging, sharing experiences, and providing training and support.[9]

Compared to other Arabic blogospheres, the number of blogs written in English is striking; Arabic is only the second most commonly used langue, followed by French. Regarding gender, according to the Berkman study of 2009, 30.2% of the Lebanese cluster are female bloggers (Etling et al., 2009: 36). To give an exact number of the current active blogs is difficult.[10] Of around 2,000 blogs, there might be up to 400 "active" blogs (that means weekly entries or more).[11] The Lebanese blogosphere is thus rather small in absolute number, but quite remarkable for the size of the country.

Lebanese bloggers

Among the most widely read and quoted blogs are those written by Lebanese in the diaspora: the *Angry Arab*,[12] *Across the Bay*[13], and *Qifa Nakbi*[14], all male Lebanese academics in the United States that offer political commentary from different angles in English.

Another predominant group are English-language blogs about Lebanon in general, which provide perspectives on daily life and politics while stressing that they are politically unbiased. One of the most frequently visited is Samer Karam's blog *Blogging Beirut*.[15] Karam has been blogging since 2005 and has played an active role in blogging on the July War of 2006. Also worth mentioning is *independence05*, which provides "thoughts and opinions from Beirut"[16],

---

8   http://lebloggers.org/
9   See for a short history of this association, see an article by one of its members, Hani Naim, in hibr journal: http://hibr.me/ar/issue4/lebaneseblogging, accessed September 17, 2010.
10 On the difficulty of measuring, see Chalhoub (2008).
11 Lebanese blogger Tony Saghbini estimates 350-400 blogs, see http://saghbini.wordpress.com/2010/08/02/, accessed August 15, 2010. This number includes mainly blogs on the platforms wordpress and blogger, but more than 2,000 registered blogs from Lebanon are to be found on the *maktoob* platform alone.
12 http://angryarab.blogspot.com/.
13 http://beirut2bayside.blogspot.com/.
14 http://qifanabki.com/.
15 http://www.bloggingbeirut.com/.
16 http:// blog.independence05.com/.

the blog *plus961*[17], which refers to the Lebanese area code, "a collection of posts about events and stuff I see in Lebanon"[18], and *Maya's Amalgam*[19], a comic blog with various social and personal stories.

Along with these there are a number of bloggers who focus on human rights and are connected with NGOs or social movements in Lebanon, for instance *Trella*, the blog by Imad Bazzi, a human rights activist and journalist, and the *Nasawiya*[20] feminist collective. There are also various leftist activists who engage in the blogosphere, link with each other, and are connected also offline. One of them is *Farfahhine*, a student and "revolutionary socialist", whose main inspiration was the activism of Egyptian bloggers,[21] and *Jou3an*, the blog by Khodor Salameh, a young Marxist.[22] They are in their early 20s and actively engaged in leftist politics in Lebanon, especially in Palestine-related issues. Like Salameh, some of them work as freelance journalists for rather leftwing journals such as *al-Akhbar* and *as-Safir*. Most of them link with *The Angry Arab* blog by As'ad Abu Khalil, the "über-leftist" (Haugbolle, 2007: 11) of the Lebanese blogosphere.[23]

Generally it can be stated that "blogging is not equally spread through Lebanon's extremely diverse political landscape" (Ward, 2007: 4), as most of the early blogosphere had close links to the demonstrations of 2005. The two main political strands represented are the March 14 coalition[24], and a spectrum of leftist and human rights activists in equal measure. The March 8 coalition is mostly absent from the blogosphere, which according to blogger Tony Saghbini might be explained by the strict form of organizations of its parties, like Hizbullah et al.[25] In sum, a general feature of the Lebanese blogosphere is that anti-sectarian views predominate and religious beliefs are rarely discussed.

....

17 http://www.plus961.com/.
18 http://www.plus961.com/about/.
19 http://mayazankoul.com/.
20 http://www.nasawiya.org/web/.
21 Interview with Farfahinne, Beirut, February 25, 2010.
22 http://farfahinne.blogspot.com/; http://jou3an.wordpress.com/.
23 As'ad Abu Khalil, political science professor at California State University, is known for critiques of media coverage of the Middle East. He is very active for the "Palestinian cause".
24 The political alliance based in these demonstrations is now called "March 14", the date of the "revolution". "March 14" is a coalition of so-called "Anti-Syrian" political parties (*Future, Lebanese Forces* et al.) and independents. "March 8" is an alliance of the opposition (*Hizbullah, Amal, Free Patriotic Movement* et al.).
25 http://saghbini.wordpress.com/2010/08/02/, accessed August 15, 2010.

B) The Egyptian Blogosphere[26]

Before 2005 there were only a few Egyptian bloggers and about 40 blogs. In this "experimentation phase" most of the bloggers were "bilingual twenty-something" and worked in computers, IT, or journalism (see Radsch, 2008: 3). They still form the core of the Egyptian blogosphere today. Most of these early blogs were written in English or in both English and Arabic.

The Egyptian blogosphere then increased from the end of 2005 on when bloggers wrote on and participated in the *Kifayah* ("enough") protests for political reform. It is doubtful that only "blogs have provided the means for Kifaya's political mobilization" (Al Malky, 2007: 4), but they certainly played a key role in the protests and, above all, they documented them in detail. At least, the emergence of the blogosphere in Egypt is strongly linked to the *Kifayah* movement. In this "activist stage", bloggers reported on protests attacked by the police and on police violence in prisons by publishing films that were recorded on mobile phones. Despite their popularity, bloggers were and are not free from repression, as the large number of imprisoned bloggers shows.[27] "International human rights organizations began regarding them as a category of social identity that could be named, invoked and politicized – they were citizen journalists" (Radsch, 2008: 5).

By 2006 the number of blogs had grown enormously and the Muslim Brothers gained a notable presence in the Egyptian blogosphere. Their blogs "resemble more the efforts of Wael Abbas' Al-Wa'i al-Masri and Manalaa.net than it [sic] does typical Brotherhood activism", states Marc Lynch (2007a: 13). They too began with a small core group of activists that expanded in 2007 and now form a distinct sub-cluster in the Egyptian blogosphere. The period from 2006 on might be labeled a "diversification phase". With the decline of the *Kifayah* movement from the end of 2006 on, the blogosphere became more diverse and fragmented and can be characterized as "a network of identity communities", as Radsch (2008: 9) suggests.

Today no single thematic focus of the Egyptian blogosphere can be identified, but some thematic fields are predominantly discussed: the lack of human

---

26 This overview is mainly based on Courney Radsch's account of "The evolution of Egypt's blogosphere" (2008).
27 For instance, Alaa Abd El Fattah (*manalalaa.net*) (Lynch, 2007a), or blogger Abdel-Kareem Nail Suleiman who was sent to prison for four years in 2007 (Al Malky, 2007: 6-7) and has been released in November 2010. Cases of harassment and arrestments are constantly being reported. See: http://threatened.globalvoicesonline.org/bloggers/egypt.

rights (torture, police violence) and women's rights in Egypt, domestic as well as international politics, and Arab-related politics, especially Palestine. The internal organization of the blogosphere reflects the political spectrum of Egypt and most of the ideological and political currents are represented. Furthermore, Egyptian youth is very engaged in blogging about a wide variety of issues, from daily life experiences with family to music and film.

In early 2007 the Egyptian blog ring counted 1,400 blogs. Meanwhile, as Manal Hassan, the woman responsible for the blog aggregator told me, the number of Egyptian blogs is about 200,000.[28] Not all of them are regularly active, but no reliable data of permanent bloggers is at hand. According to a study from 2008, 73% of the bloggers were male and 27% female (IDSC, 2008).

Egyptian bloggers[29]

Presenting an overview of the huge number of Egyptian bloggers is impossible, so I will focus on the political or activist blogs. One powerful group within the blogosphere is the political and human rights activists from the wider opposition, who especially in the beginning of blogging were closely connected. Just to mention two of the best-known: Wael Abbas with his blog *al-Wa'i al-Masri*[30] (Egyptian awareness) is a leading example of publishing videos of police violence in Egypt. He is a journalist and human rights activist who became internationally recognized through various international awards[31] and interviews in mainstream media related to politics in Egypt. Another famous blog is *3arabawy*[32], maintained by Hossam el-Hamalawy, a journalist and socialist activist, who covers all kinds of workers strikes and protests worldwide. The blog is written in Arabic and English and provides many links to newspaper articles from *al-Masry al-Youm*, *Daily News*, etc. or to other blogs like *The Angry Arab*.

---

28 Personal communication from Manal Hassan at the *Second Arab Bloggers Meeting* on December 11, 2010 in Beirut. Together with her husband Alaa Abd El Fattah, she is responsible for the Egyptian blog aggregator.
29 Mainly based on Etling et al. (2009). For a critical comment on the study's categorization of bloggers, see Syrian blogger Razan: http://razanghazzawi.com/2009/08/14/berkman-centers-study-of-the-arab-blogphere-map-terminology/, accessed December 12, 2010.
30 http://misrdigital.blogspirit.com/.
31 Human Rights Watch in 2008, *Knight International Journalism award* in 2007; he was as also named the most influential activist in 2006 by the BBC.
32 http://arabist.net/arabawy/author/hossam/.

A second distinctive group is the Muslim Brothers bloggers (Etling et al., 2009: 4), who write predominantly in Arabic.[33] Like the first group, they advocate freedom of speech in Egypt. The best-known blog is *Ana Ikhwan*[34] (which translates as "I am the Brotherhood") by Abd Al Moneim Mahmoud, a 29-year-old journalist working for *ikhwan.web*, the Brotherhood's website. In his blog he comments on domestic and Arab politics, as well as on Islam-related issues. Despite the title and his self-identification with the Brotherhood, he writes in the blog's header that it is "only expressing my opinion independently". Other examples include *2mwag*, "Waves in the sea of change"[35], a blogger collective of 16 bloggers, active since September 2007, and blogger Abdel Rahman Ayyash, who has both a blog in Arabic and one in English.[36] Within his blog he is trying to "show good model of a young Egyptian Muslim guy, who is believing in Islam as the only solution to all problems we face". Links common to these blogs are the Brotherhood's website *ikhwan.web* and the Islamic web portal *islam.online* (Gräf, 2008).

Aside of these, there is a wide range of blogs that are not clearly political, such as *Baheyya*, *Egyptian Chronicles*, and *Lasto Adri*.[37] They provide political commentary, engage in current discussions, and also write rather personal stories. *Kolenaleila*[38], a project initiated by *Lasto Adri* and other bloggers, publishes various stories about women's life in Egypt and now also other Arab countries.

2   Counterpublics

On the basis of these two cases, I will now turn to the theoretical background of my paper: the counterpublics concept. I will first outline Fraser's notion of subaltern counterpublics and some further discussions of her concept. Following up on this, I will raise some questions concerning its transfer to a special media form on the internet.

---

33 See Lynch (2007b).
34 http://ana-ikhwan.blogspot.com/.
35 http://2mwag.blogspot.com/.
36 al-ghareeb.blogspot.com, http://2-b-egyptian.blogspot.com/.
37 http://baheyya.blogspot.com/, http://egyptianchronicles.blogspot.com/, http://lasto-adri.blogspot.com/.
38 http://kolenalaila.com/.

Theoretical Background

Nancy Fraser's article "Rethinking the Public Sphere: A Contribution to the Critique of Actually Existing Democracy" is probably the most prominent contribution to the theory of counterpublics, and several scholars have been working with this concept or extending it. The article was published in an edited volume on *Habermas and the Public Sphere* (1992) in which various scholars provide a critical review of the Habermasian bourgeois public sphere from 1962 (English translation 1989). Fraser's article is to be read as a critical engagement with Habermas' public sphere concept from a feminist perspective. Her conceptualization of a "plurality of competing publics" counters Habermas' idea of a single public sphere. She argues for a critical interrogation of his idealized concept, discussing mainly gender and class exclusions. Her argument is that the bourgeois was never *the* public and that "competing counterpublics" existed as women's public arenas (Fraser, 1992: 116). The emphasis in her approach lies on the contestatory function of subaltern counterpublics – which is not undisputed. For example, Jodi Dean criticizes that such "publics" are merely groups, because they have special concerns and are partial (Dean, 2003: 97). But for Fraser, despite their function of "withdrawal and regroupment" (Fraser, 1992: 116), these arenas are *publics*, as they have a publicist orientation and in their "agitational activities" are directed toward wider publics (Fraser, 1992: 124).

Fraser refers to alternative publics in stratified societies as "subaltern counterpublics in order to signal that they are parallel discursive arenas where members of subordinated social groups invent and circulate counterdiscourses to formulate oppositional interpretations of their identities, interests, and needs" (Fraser, 1992: 123). This definition of a counterpublic presupposes that the actors of this public are "subalterns" or "subordinated groups" that formulate "oppositional interpretations" of their own interests, etc.

One critical engagement with the Fraserian concept that can be made useful in this context is Michael Warner's "Publics and Counterpublics" (2002). In his work on queer counterpublics in the last three centuries, Warner complicates the notion by raising the question of the ways one might be subaltern. His argument is that the reasons why members of a certain public might be regarded as subaltern can differ greatly and that sometimes mere participation in a certain public can make people subaltern (Warner, 2002: 87). Concerning the question of what the public is actually "countering" or addressing, he explains: "A counterpublic maintains at some level, conscious or not, an awareness of its subordinate status. The cultural horizon against which it marks itself off is not just a general or wider public, but a dominant one. And the conflict extends not just to ideas or policy questions, but to the speech genres and modes of address that constitute the public and to the hierarchy among media." (Warner, 2002: 86) Shedding light on these different modes of address is a useful perspective for research on counterpublics.

Overall, even if discussed critically by some scholars, the Fraserian concept still provides the most useful framework for understanding counterpublics.[39] By arguing for a model of multiple publics that does not contradict the public sphere concept, it challenges other public sphere theories and theorists.

Counterpublics on the Internet?

But can one apply this framework to blogs, a special media format on the internet? In his book *Zero comments: Blogging and critical internet culture* (2007), Geert Lovink provides a critical (re-)vision of the media format and states right at the beginning: "Blogs zero out centralized meaning structures and focus on personal experiences – not, primarily, news media" (Lovink, 2007: 1). But from his point of view, this does not mean that they necessarily express oppositional interpretations. Lovink criticizes that "blogs have been discussed mainly in oppositional terms, as being a counter-voice to the dominant news industry" while "the blogging majority is conservative" (ibid). Even if his study focuses more on blogging in Western Europe and America, it is important to keep in mind that blogging is not per se a "counter-voice". But it needs to be added that in some contexts a conservative voice may also be politically oppositional, for example a religious conservative blogger in Egypt.

Thus, the media format as such does not lead to the formation of a counterpublic. It can be regarded as a new possibility of participation in public discussion (Benkler, 2006)[40] just as well as another part of the internet's "contestatory network" (Dean, 2003)[41] in which, in the best case, groups of like-minded people discuss with each other.

---

39 For an extended presentation of the "Begriffsgeschichte" of counterpublics, see Wimmer 2007.
40 Benkler argues in *Wealth of Networks* (2006) that the internet leads to a "qualitative change in the role of individuals as potential investigators and commentators, as active participants in defining the agenda and debating action in the public sphere" (Benkler, 2006: 225).
41 Dean (2003) criticizes the new media's self-representation as a democratic public.

Another objection to applying the concept of the counterpublic to blogging is that the structure of publics from the late 20th century feminist counterpublic in the United States – through which Fraser exemplified her theory – to contemporary internet-based communication has changed quite a lot. This already becomes evident if we examine two aspects: first, temporality on the internet is structured in a different way than in traditional print media, in which circulation is organized mainly in predefined rhythms. Publication and reception on the internet have become simultaneous processes and "highly mediated and highly capitalized forms of circulation are increasingly organized as continuous ('24/7 Instant Access') rather than punctual" (Warner, 2002: 68-69). According to Warner, this "absence of punctual rhythms may make it very difficult to connect localized acts of reading to the modes of agency that prevail within the social imaginary of modernity" (ibid: 69). Second, blogging is at the same time a local and a translocal media practice, in terms of its producers as well as its readers. This means that the notion of the "general public" cannot be taken for granted, because who or what the general public is thought to be and who is addressed may differ from blog to blog: whether a local or national public, a regional one, a translocal public, up to a "world" public.[42] Fraser's critique, however, "presupposed the national-territorial understanding of publicity" (Fraser, 2007).[43]

All this shows that the transfer of the concept of the (counter)public to the internet and blogging in particular is not an easy fit and additional theoretical concepts are necessary. Useful approaches may be those focusing on the network character of internet publics, for instance Castell's "network society" (1996) or Anderson's approach to blogging in the Middle East as a "networked public" (2009). But overall, in my opinion the analysis of case studies is the most promising way to develop new theoretical insights.

With these theoretical considerations in mind, I will now come back to my case studies for a comparative look at three aspects of the blogospheres that are relevant for the question of counterpublic: (A) the actors' backgrounds and position in society, (B) who they actually address, and (C) the causes in which they engage. The first question refers to the "subaltern"-ness of the actors, which both Fraser and Warner emphasize. The last two questions are inspired

---

[42] For a discussion on the internet and the change in the public sphere, see Bucher (2002). For translocality as an analytical category, see Freitag/von Oppen 2010.

[43] In this more recent article, Fraser discusses whether the public sphere theory is still useful for analyzing current "transnational publics (Fraser, 2007).

by Warner's notion of "modes of address", which I want to discuss regarding language use (B) and by looking at different causes bloggers engage in (C).

3 Actors, Audiences, Causes

A) Bloggers' Backgrounds

Fraser defines counterpublics as publics in which "subordinated social groups" "invent and circulate counterdiscourses" (Fraser, 2007) and Warner mentions the awareness of the "subaltern status" (2002: 86) in the counterpublic as an essential feature. But are the actors in this field subordinated or subaltern in any way?

Looking at the profiles of the most widely read Lebanese bloggers, one easily notices that a lot of them are academics, journalists, IT workers, and knowledge workers in general. The majority of bloggers has obtained higher education, which usually implies English-language education. Blogging in Lebanon is therefore to be described as a middle- and upper-class activity. Access[44] to the internet is limited, because the infrastructure in Lebanon is not well developed, which leads to high prices and slow internet connections.[45] Regarding social background, Lebanese bloggers are rather privileged in their society. Nevertheless, a lot of bloggers may be regarded as subalterns because of the political or religious (or rather non-religious) views that they express or their sexual orientation. A blogging radical leftist, a homosexual, or an atheist holds views that strongly oppose dominant values in their society.

Concerning Egypt, one can argue in a similar vein. As mentioned before, the first bloggers in Egypt often had a background in IT or journalism, and this is still common for the blogosphere. Today, as the technical entry barrier into the blogosphere has become lower and internet access has grown[46], the

---

44 Reliable data on internet access and use is hardly accessible. This is partly due to self-reported internet use and also to the sharing of personal computers, which are difficult to measure. *Internetworldstats* reports one million internet users in June 2010 for Lebanon, or about 24.2 % of the population (see internetworldstats.com/middle.htm#lb).

45 Maha Taki holds the political and economic conditions in Lebanon responsible for the low internet penetration, as there is a "lack of developed infrastructure" (Taki, 2008: 284).

46 According to *internetworldstats* Egypt had 17,060,000 internet users in February 2010, which means 21.2 % of the population used the internet (see internetworldstats.com/Africa.htm#eg). The number of users alone is outstanding in the Arab

overall blogger scene includes bloggers with a wide variety of backgrounds. Still, the majority of bloggers and of internet users have some university education (Abdulla, 2007: 50). But even more than in Lebanon, bloggers in Egypt have a subaltern status because of their political oppositional opinions or their expressed religious identity as Baheyyas, Copts, or atheists. Furthermore, following Warner it could be argued that simply belonging to the Egyptian blogosphere imparts a subaltern status and risks oppression that one would not otherwise face.

Nevertheless, blogging as such is not to be regarded as a subaltern activity. Bloggers also use their blogs for their own professionalization as designers or writers. And bloggers may also belong to dominant groups and express corresponding views, whether political or social. So the notion of the subaltern who is aware of his or her subordinate status (see Warner 2002: 86) does fit certain bloggers, but surely not the blogosphere as a whole.

B) Ways of Addressing: Language

A first aspect of ways of addressing is surely language. Language use is also one of the major differences between the Lebanese and Egyptian blogosphere. This issue deserves more detailed study, since language use and politics in both countries (dialects, use of foreign languages, etc.) are quite complex, but I would still like to engage in some preliminary reflections on the reasons for this difference.

In the Lebanese blogosphere, English is the predominant language and used by the majority of A-list bloggers. It is followed by Arabic and then French. Some bloggers use both languages alternately or even have two different blogs.[47] Others also post in both languages or understand themselves as a bridge between the two languages and their audiences – as for example *Ethiopian suicides*[48], an issue blog focusing on migrant domestic workers in Lebanon.

The use of English "allows bloggers to communicate with international human rights groups, media, researchers, and, most importantly, a community

---

world. Egypt belongs to the states with the highest growth rates in the Arab world and is the first when it comes to the amount of data transferred (Abdulla, 2007: 39).

47 Like *Ana Min Beirut*: http://anaminbeirut.blogspot.com/ and http://minbeirutbilarabeh.blogspot.com/
48 http://www.ethiopiansuicides.blogspot.com/.

of other bloggers worldwide" (Haugbolle, 2007: 4). The Lebanese blogosphere, at least in its beginnings, was very much an endeavor of academics, researchers, and political analysts that provided political analysis for an informed public in both Lebanon and abroad. It is especially these early bloggers that fit the category of bridge bloggers, i.e., bloggers who "primarily address Western audiences, usually writing an English with the intention of explaining their societies" (Lynch, 2007a: 11). This outreach and bridging factor is partly related to the huge Lebanese diaspora, which is estimated to be up to 15 million people and thus much larger than the population in Lebanon, which amounts to approximately four million people. Another reason to use English might be the bloggers' backgrounds, as described above. Since most of them obtained higher education in English, using this language often seems "natural" and is not even questioned, as I noticed during my fieldwork. Typing Arabic even poses a problem for some of the bloggers; they are often more used to typing in English or French. Still, there are a number of bloggers who post in Arabic, for example most of the leftist bloggers, but also bloggers who are not clearly politically affiliated. They explain this by their choice of audience: they want communicate primarily with Lebanese or Arabs in general. Still, this issue deserves more detailed study, because language is highly contested in Lebanon, as is revealed in current discussion about the state of Arabic in Lebanon.[49]

In the Egyptian blogosphere, by contrast, the percentage of Arabic blogs, whether in standard Arabic or the Egyptian dialect, is much higher. Since its beginning, the Egyptian blogosphere was more related to activism "on the spot". Even if blogs also provided reports for foreign media, the most important audience seems to be Egyptians themselves. To inform them about the situation in Egypt is a goal of Wael Abbas' blog "Egyptian awareness", for example. Wael Abbas explained to me that he writes in English only when he seeks international solidarity, but mostly writes in Arabic because his blog targets primarily young Egyptians.[50] Of course one cannot generalize about the overall blogosphere on the basis of one "star blogger", but generally speaking a focus on local readership seems to be a common trend and much stronger than in the Lebanese case.

---

49 http://beirutspring.com/blog/2010/03/01/hi-kifak-ca-va-pride/.
50 Interview with Wael Abbas at the *Second Arab Bloggers Meeting* in Beirut, December 9, 2009.

Nevertheless, also for Egyptian bloggers it is not always "natural" to blog in Arabic, since many of them, too, obtained an English-language education and are more used to writing in English. For example, the *Lasto Adri* blogger told me that some Egyptian bloggers encouraged her to change her blog to Arabic and that she therefore worked a lot on her Arabic writing skills.[51] And there are also a number of bloggers who post in English as *Egyptian Chronicles*; they should be considered bridge bloggers.

Who is addressed is, of course, not only a matter of language, but also of styles of writing. Those styles are quite diverse in blogging: newspaper-like political commentary, poetry, the use of dialect and everyday language, and all kinds of nonstandard speech, to name just a few. Informality, as Sune Haugbolle (2007) points out, applies to form as well as to content; different languages might be mixed, grammar and spelling changed, capital letters omitted, and so forth. Linking, whether to other blogs or to different channels like *YouTube*, and *Facebook*, and *Twitter*, are also active ways of addressing audiences.

To sum up, language use indicates that the Lebanese blogosphere is more oriented toward a translocal public, whereas the Egyptian is more concentrated on the local audience and its mobilization.

C) Causes: What Bloggers Engage in

Whom or what does the blogosphere or sub-public challenge? What are the causes bloggers engage in? And which public is respectively addressed? I would like to shed some more light on the causes or events bloggers mobilize for and present two events in the history of each blogosphere. These do not represent all activities in the blogosphere, but rather point to differences in how counterpublics in the blogosphere are evolving and how they are structured.

Lebanon 1: During the July War of 2006, a lot of bloggers felt the responsibility to write about what was happening or needed a channel to express what they were experiencing. In their blog posts, the writers challenged an international version of the event in which Lebanon (*Hizbullah*) was often portrayed

---

51 Interview with *Lasto Adri* blogger at the *Second Arab Bloggers Meeting* in Beirut, December 9, 2009.

as the responsible party and countered it with personal stories[52] or analysis "on the spot". They were actively engaged in providing another representation of the war, documenting the consequences for the civil population, and calling for an end to the Israeli military assaults.

Often the blogs began as notes for friends, to inform them about the current situation, but then turned into providing "alternative" news for a much broader public.[53] The blogosphere was not mainly countering the national public in Lebanon but vastly transcending its boundaries. Most of these blogs were written in English or French, so they were able to reach an international public: a public that was no longer to be localized, but truly translocal. This moment was surely unique in the history of the Lebanese blogosphere. Even if many blogs stopped after the war, the event was a catalyst for blogging activity and showed its momentary force.

Lebanon 2: A second, more recent example from the Lebanese blogosphere is the blogging about the demonstrations against the Egyptian wall on the Egypt/Gaza Strip border in front of the Egyptian embassy in Beirut on January 26, 2010. Some leftist bloggers[54] were active first in mobilizing and then in reporting on this demonstration. The event became a distinctive moment in the blogosphere, because various bloggers shared their blog posts[55] or got to know about each other's respective blogging activity. During the demonstration, the army attacked some protesters and the bloggers provided photos, films, and reports on this particular part of the event. In the aftermath, some bloggers wrote articles in which they severely criticized the army as such.[56] Only one Lebanese channel (*New TV*) and one newspaper (*al-Akhbar*) covered the army's attacks.[57] Most of the involved bloggers wrote in Arabic, while only a few English posts were published.[58] This indicates that primarily a local and regional (Arabic-speaking) public was targeted.

---

52 See *Muzna's stories*, now on http://hakaya.blogspot.com/.
53 See for example Rasha Salti's blog: http://rashasalti.blogspot.com/2006/07/lebanon-siege-day-5.html, accessed March 25, 2010.
54 http://farfahinne.blogspot.com; http://hanzala.wordpress.com; jou3an.wordpress.com; http://beirutiyat.wordpress.com; http://hanibaael.wordpress; http://saghbini.wordpress.com.
55 See http://hanibaael.wordpress.com/2010/01/25/, accessed January 30, 2010.
56 Jou3an on January 24 and 26 (no longer accessible) and Hanzala on January 25: http://hanzala86.blogspot.com/2010/01/blog-post.html, accessed March 25, 2010. Part of Hanzala's article was published in Al-Akhbar.
57 Interview with Khodor Salameh on January 24, 2010 and blogger Farfahinne on February 25, 2010.
58 Farfahinne, for example, published an English post of a "comrade": http://farfahinne.

Egypt 1: A series of sexual assaults in Cairo in October 2006 became a defining moment for the Egyptian blogosphere. During the religious holiday Eid al-Fitr, young women were harassed in downtown Cairo Downtown without any interference from the police (Radsch, 2008). Bloggers were around the corner to document the assaults and published them on their blogs[59], which were heavily visited, especially since the state-run media did not report on the event. It took some days before the story migrated to the daily *al-Masry al-Youm, al-Dustour*, and other newspapers. This was one of the few examples in which the stories of the blogs really made it to the Egyptian mainstream media.

Egypt 2: Torture has been one of the main fields bloggers report on. Wael Abbas' blog *al-Wa'i al-Masri* is a leading example of publishing videos of police violence in Egypt. One of the most prominent cases is from 2007, when he published a video of police beating, torturing, and sexually abusing a bus driver with an iron stick, an incident that had happened in 2006. This led to a court case in which two police officers were sentenced. The case attracted media attention in Egypt as well as internationally (*Le Figaro, Libération, The Guardian*, etc.[60]) and is one of the success stories against police violence in Egypt. Nevertheless, after this case, the media tend to be less interested in such cases, as Abbas criticized in an interview in 2009.[61] What is striking in this instance is that the video had been public before on *YouTube*, but was not framed in the same way.[62] This shows how same information can be perceived in different ways and that publishing per se does not make the case, but framing certain actions as injustice does. Abbas and his fellow bloggers have constantly challenged the Egyptian regime by exposing structural injustice that has not been prosecuted, and on another level they have increased Egyptians' awareness of torture.[63] The addressed audience of such exposures consists

---

blogspot.com/2010/01/police-attack-protestors-at-egyptian.html, accessed March 25, 2010.

59 See Malek Mostafa on http://malek-x.net/node/268, accessed September 17, 2010 (Al Malky, 2007 for a detailed study of the event).
60 See http://misrdigital.blogspirit.com/archive/2007/01/index.html, accessed March 25, 2010.
61 http://www.menassat.com/?q=en/news-articles/7111-egyptian-blogger-uncovers-new-alleged-case-police-torture.
62 This was mentioned in a discussion about blogging in Egypt with Wael Abbas, Alaa Abd El Fattah, and Manal Hassan at the *Second Arab Bloggers Meeting* 2009, Beirut, December 11, 2009.
63 See also Noha Atef's blog: http://www.tortureinegypt.net/.

mainly of Egyptians themselves. Another audience is of course the international public and press, which can help pressure the Egyptian regime.

In summary it can be stated, that different oppositional views are expressed in these two blogospheres. In Egypt, the state is challenged as police violence and torture are exposed and the non-democratic regime constantly criticized. Egypt is one of the countries with the highest number of arrested bloggers, which clearly shows that the government does not tolerate such views. Oppositional views are expressed in Lebanon, as well, but on another level. In general, the sectarian political system and politics are often criticized, especially by Leftist bloggers. But as a whole, the Lebanese blogosphere is not as politicized and related to activism as the Egyptian one is.

Concrete cases from Lebanon and Egypt reveal varying forms of counterpublics on the internet; they challenge different representations and target different audiences: a rather "global public" (Bucher, 2002: 514ff.) or translocal networked public in the Lebanon war and a local and regional public in the demonstration against the Egyptian wall in Gaza. In Egypt, the main target is the local public and international coverage is seen as a support in special cases. This shows that both the local and international media context must be taken into consideration if we are to fully grasp the dynamics of counterpublics on the internet. One feature of "translocal media cultures" (see Hepp, 2002) is how certain "news" travels between local and international media.

4   Preliminary Answers and Further Thoughts

The Fraserian concept, rooted in a specific time and a US context, has limited applicability. The analysis of two specific Middle Eastern blogospheres revealed it to be too static to provide a meaningful understanding of the dynamics between blogging and the wider public sphere. Nevertheless, the concept (and its extensions by Warner) have proven to be a useful tool for generating questions to analyze specific blogospheres. A look at the background, the addressees, and the cases of engagement makes heterogeneous forms of counterpublics visible. Overall, no distinctive stable "subaltern counterpublic" in the Fraserian sense can be made out in either blogosphere. Rather, we see temporary issue publics, as during the high of the Egyptian *kifayah* movement or in the July War of 2006 in Lebanon. Sub-publics in the blogospheres seem to be able to form counterpublics for a special cause and a limited time. Blogs are efficient framers of new issues (like police violence and sexual harassment).

It is important to consider convergence with other media forms, because blogs do not "act" in an autonomous field, but are strongly interlinked with other media forms on the internet (*YouTube, Twitter*) and in "offline" publications. In Lebanon one finds extension of other sub-publics in the blogosphere: there is a Lebanese leftist public that extends into the blogosphere, which is reflected by the links between and common actors in *al-Akhbar, as-Safir,* and certain blogs. In the Egyptian blogosphere, we see several interrelated counterpublic spheres, like that of the Muslim Brothers (with special links to *ikhwan.online*) or of bloggers from the wider opposition with links to other media like *al-Masry al-Youm* and *ad-Dustour*.

In addition, despite the national bounds of the blogospheres, production and reception are translocal phenomena (especially in the Lebanese case). As shown above, which audience is addressed changes depending on the cause and the actors. For this reason, different publics, local, regional, translocal, and global must be taken into consideration. A challenge for this kind of research is that blogosphere publics constantly change and are not stable entities.

Finally, it has to be questioned what the wider or "dominant public" is at all. Whereas in Egypt it might be the public loyal to the regime, in the segmented society of Lebanon, it is hard to distinguish a dominant public at all. Ongoing research and theoretical reflection are needed to grasp the internal dynamics of these blogospheres and to evaluate their relation to national publics and wider public spheres. The classical concept of public sphere versus counterpublic(s) does not sufficiently capture the contemporary dynamics within the fragmentation of publics.

Bibliography

ABDULLA, R. A., 2007. *The Internet in the Arab World: Egypt and Beyond.* New York et al.: Lang.

ANDERSON, J., 2009. Another Free-Speech Panacea for the Middle East?, *NMIT Working Papers*, [online] Available at: http://nmit.wordpress.com/2009/01/31/197/ [Accessed 31 January 2010].

ARMBRUST, W., 2007. New Media and Old Agendas: The Internet in the Middle East and Middle Eastern Studies, *International Journal of Middle Eastern Studies*, 39 (4), pp. 531-533.

BAYM, N. K. & MARKHAM, A. N., 2009. *Internet Inquiry: Conversations about Method.* Los Angeles et al.: Sage.

BENKLER, Y., 2006. *The Wealth of Networks: How Social Production Transforms Markets and Freedom.* New Haven: Yale University Press.

BUCHER, H. J., 2002. Internet und globale Kommunikation: Ansätze eines Strukturwandels der Öffentlichkeit. In: M. LÖFFELHOLZ & A. HEPP, ed. *Grundlagentexte zur Transkulturellen Kommunikation.* Constance: UVK, pp. 500-530.

CALHOUN, C., ed., 1992. *Habermas and the Public Sphere.* Cambridge et al.: MIT Press.

CASTELL, M., 1996. *The Rise of the Network Society.* Malden MA: Blackwell.

CHALHOUB, N., 2008. Mesurer la société de l'information dans le monde arabe: de la difficulté d'une nécessité. In: Y. GONZALES-QUIJANO AND C. VARIN, ed., *La société de l'information au Proche-Orient.* Beirut: Université Saint Joseph, CEMAM, pp. 19-37.

DAHLGREN, P., 2005. The Internet, Public Spheres, and Political Communication: Dispersion and Liberation. *Political Communication*, 22 (2), pp. 147-162.

DEAN, J., 2003. Why the Net is not a Public Sphere. *Constellations*, 1 (1), pp. 95-112.

ETLING, B. & KELLY, J. & FARIS, R. & PALFREY, J., 2009. Mapping The Arab Blogosphere: Politics, Culture, and Dissent., *Internet and Democracy Project*, [online] Available at: http://cyber.law.harvard.edu/publications/2009/Mapping_the_Arabic_Blogosphere [Accessed 8 January 2010].

FRASER, N., 1992. Rethinking the Public Sphere: A Contribution to the Critique of Actually Existing Democracy. In: C. CALHOUN, ed. *Habermas and the Public Sphere.* Cambridge et al.: MIT Press, pp. 109-142.

FRASER, N., 2007. Transnationalizing the Public Sphere: On the Legitimacy and Efficacy of Public Opinion in a Post-Westphalian World. *Theory, Culture & Society*, 24 (4), pp. 7-30, also [online] Available at: http://eipcp.net/transversal/0605/fraser/en [Accessed 21 September 2010].

FREITAG, U. & VON OPPEN, A., 2010. Introduction: 'Translocality': An Approach to Connection and Transfer in Area Studies. In: FREITAG, U. & VON OPPEN, A., ed. *Translocality: The Study of Globalising Processes from a Southern Perspective.* Leiden: Brill, pp. 1-21.

GRÄF, B., 2008. IslamOnline.net: Interactive, Independent, Popular, *Arab Media and Society*, 4 (2008), [online] Available at: http://www.arabmediasociety.com/?article=576 [Accessed 22 September 2010].

HAUGBOLLE, S., 2007. From A-lists to Webtifadas: Developments in the Lebanese Blogosphere 2005-2006, *Arab Media & Society*, 1 (2007), [online] Available at: http://arabmediasociety.sqgd.co.uk/topics/index.php?t_article=91 [Accessed 10 March 2009].

HEPP, A., 2002. Translokale Medienkulturen. In: A. HEPP & M. LÖFFELHOLZ, ed. *Grundlagentexte zur Transkulturellen Kommunikation*, Constance: UVK, pp. 861-885.

IDSC (Information and Decision Support Center), 2008. *Al- Mudawwanat al-Misriya: Fada' ijtima'i jaded*, [online] Available at: http:/www.idsc.gov.eg/upload/ Publications/blogs%20final-2.pdf [Accessed 8 March 2009].

KLAUS, E., 2009. The Integration of Weblogs in the Egyptian Media Environment. In: A. HEINEMANN & O. LAMLOUM & A. FRANCOIS, ed. *The Middle East in the Media: Conflicts, Censorship and Public Opinion*. London: Saqi Books, pp. 252-267.

LOVINK, G., 2007. *Zero Comments: Blogging and Critical Internet Culture*. New York: Routledge.

LYNCH, M., 2007a. Blogging the New Arab Public, *Arab Media & Society*, 1 (2007), [online] Available at: http://arabmediasociety.sqgd.co.uk/topics/ index.php?t_article=32 [Accessed 7 August 2009].

LYNCH, M., 2007b. Young Brothers in Cyberspace, *Middle East Report*, 245 (2007), [online] Available at: http://www.merip.org/mer/mer245/lynch.html [Accessed 10 September 2010].

AL MALKY, R., 2007. Blogging for Reform: The Case of Egypt, *Arab Media & Society*, 1 (2007), [online] Available at: http://www.arabmediasociety.com/topics/ index.php?t_article=39 [Accessed 8 January 2009].

Ó BAOILL, A., 2004. Weblogs and the Public Sphere. In: L. GURAK ET AL., ed. *Into the Blogosphere: Rhetoric, Community, and Culture of Weblogs*, [online] Available at: http://blog.lib.umn.edu/blogosphere/weblogs_and_the_public_sphere.html [Accessed 31 August 2009].

RADSCH, C. A., 2008. Core to Commonplace: The Evolution of Egypt's Blogosphere, *Arab Media and Society*, 6 (2008), [online] Available at: http://www.arabmediasociety.com/topics/index.php?t_article=228 [Accessed 7 August 2009].

TAKI, M., 2008. The Demise of 'Virtuality': A Case Study of Weblogs in Lebanon and Syria. In: N. CARPENTIER ET AL., ed. *Democracy, Journalism and Technology: New Developments in an Enlarged Europe*. University of Tartu Press, pp. 281-292.

WARD, W., 2007. Uneasy Bedfellows: Bloggers and Mainstream Media Report the Lebanon conflict, *Arab Media and Society*, 1 (2007), [online] Available at: http://www.arabmediasociety.com/topics/index.php?t_article=52 [Accessed 10 March 2008].

WARNER, M., 2002. Publics and Counterpublics. *Public Culture*, 14 (1), pp. 49-90.

WIMMER, J., 2007. *(Gegen-)Öffentlichkeit in der Mediengesellschaft: Analyse eines medialen Spannungsverhältnisses*. Wiesbaden: VS.

Fritzi-Marie Titzmann

Medialisation and Social Change – The Indian Online Matrimonial Market as a New Field of Research

Introduction

For centuries Indian families sought help from relatives, marriage brokers and later newspaper advertisements to marry their sons and daughters off. They relied on kinship and caste networks, on marriage bureaus and on "word of mouth". However, the global media age has opened up a whole new world of possibilities and renders a new dimension to the Indian matrimonial market's medialisation. The first India-based websites dedicated to matrimonial matchmaking appeared on the World Wide Web in the late 1990s and the number of users has increased ever since. These websites provide a complex picture of young Indians searching for partners for life. A detailed analysis of the matrimonial profiles offers a remarkable insight into the changing concepts of marriage, love and gender roles. The sheer fact that millions of profiles containing personal information are accessible via the Internet proves how significant the medialisation[1] aspect is. Media permeate very intimate and personal domains, thus becoming part of social change. Hepp has developed an approach of medial moulding forces of social and cultural change in which he defines three key dimensions for medialisation: individualization as social tendency, deterritorialization with regard to space and increasing immediacy as temporal dimension (Hepp, 2010). His approach serves as an excellent starting point for the analysis, but with regard to the complex dynamics of the Indian online matrimonial market, it also requires further refinement.

India's matrimonial market can be seen as paradigmatic for the medialisation process. On the one hand, marriage as a central social event is being medialised. On the other hand, changing gender roles, social concepts and

---

1 Medialisation or "mediatization" is currently discussed in divergent ways as a meta process of socio cultural change. Basically the term describes an increasing influence of communication media into different social and cultural spheres (See Hepp, 2010; Hepp, 2009; Kim, 2008; Bergmann, 2006).

values are being reflected in design and advertisements as well as the user profiles, thus providing information into social change. A new immediacy through technological progress in communication can be observed as well. Contacting prospective brides or grooms is much quicker and time-saving through the internet, by email or mobile phone than using the services of marriage bureaus or newspapers. Simultaneously, the exploration of Indian matrimonial websites overlaps with multiple other issues. The global Indian online matrimonial market includes a strong transnational component which deserves special attention. Deterritorialization is definitely a key factor here, but Hepp's concept doesn't take into consideration that the processes of localization and regionalisation take place simultaneously. With regards to gender-related debates, matrimonial websites are interesting sources for the construction and mediation processes of feminity. However, consisting of global or transnational media products, the Indian online matrimonial market in its cultural specificity is first of all a social phenomenon anchored in India, including its widespread diaspora. Thus it is definitely a relevant subject for area studies on the region. Despite the fact that most of the online matchmaking sites are in English[2], a comprehensive understanding and analysis would not be fruitful without any prior knowledge of the region and its particular social, cultural and religious stratification and diversity. Area expertise is a crucial factor if one wants to detect cultural change without perpetuating stereotypes.

In this paper, I will discuss two aspects derived from an in-depth analysis of 200 profiles and a series of interviews conducted with matrimonial website users in Mumbai, 2008, and analyse the afore-mentioned aspect of transnational representations of feminity:
1. The dichotomy in arranged marriages versus love marriages
2. The change in partner expectations and the negotiation of family-oriented and individual requirements within the process of searching a partner.

Using these examples, I intend to show how much potential this field of research provides despite being so far widely ignored in the academic sphere. There is very limited research literature on matrimonial print advertisement in

---

2 Some of the websites are available in India's regional languages.

India (see Shukla and Kapadia, 2007; Majumdar, 2004; Sharda, 1990; Rao and Rao, 1990; Choudhury and Choudhury and Mohanty, 1995; Banerjee, 2009). Hardly any work contains more than one reference to online matrimonials (Hankeln, 2008). Exceptions are Seth and Patnayakuni's (2009) "Online matrimonial sites and the transformations of arranged marriage in India" as well as Sharma's (2008) "Caste on Indian Marriage dot-com: Presence and Absence", which focuses exclusively on the Indian diaspora in North America. Sharangpani's article "Browsing for Bridegrooms: Matchmaking and Modernity in Mumbai" offers an insight into modern matchmaking practices and media (Sharangpani, 2010). Equally worth mentioning is Jha and Adelman's study on the significance of skin colour in the Indian online matrimonial market (Jha and Adelman, 2009). Apart from that, the majority of the existing literature is rather popular or anecdotic and gives merely a first impression (Pepper, 2007). In view of the state of research, a deeper examination of the Indian online matrimonial market is worthwhile.

The Indian Online Matrimonial Market

The rise of online matrimonial websites is part of a general boom that has taken place in the Indian media landscape since the 1990s with economic liberalization and privatization (Munshi, 2001: 79; Schneider, 2007). The exact number of online matrimonial websites is currently unclear but rough calculations find about 2500 – half of which are Indian, or at least South Asian (Kaur, 2002). This is not surprising. Marriage arrangements through newspaper advertisements, marriage bureaus and family networks have a long-lasting tradition in South Asia. The Internet is only one more medium used to simplify the search of a partner. India is not called the new IT nation without reason. The growing number of young educated computer users fluent in English explains the overwhelming response matrimonial websites are getting. Overall, India's 38 million Internet users make up the world's fourth largest group of online users (IAMAI's Report on Matrimonial Search '2006': 2). According to a study conducted by the Internet and Mobile Association of India, about 80 percent of the users of matrimonial websites are between 18 and 35 years old, have at least a college degree and live in one of India's mega-cities.[3] The study finds a rapid and continuous rise in user numbers since 2005. It estimates that there were about 7 million users of matrimonial websites in 2006 and 2007 (IAMAI's Report on Matrimonial Search '2006': 2).

The online matrimonial market is led by three main websites: Shaadi.com, BharatMatrimony.com and Jeevansathi.com[4] whereby Shaadi.com claims the highest number of users and successful matches. Shaadi.com's biggest competitor is BharatMatrimony.com, which has developed a different business strategy by going mainly with regional affiliations. The portal consists of 15 regional sub-sites, called TamilMatrimony, BengalMatrimony, MarathiMatrimony etc. BharatMatrimony.com has a stronger hold in South India (Pepper, 2007). In comparison to Shaadi.com, Jeevansathi.com seems to attract fewer Non-Resident Indians (NRI's) and educated urban candidates, and is consequently rated as less effective by many of my interviewees. Apart from these big websites, there are a vast number of small sites which attract plenty of subscribers: Indianmatrimonials.com, Pyar.org, lifepartnerindia.com, matrisearch.com, merasathi.com. New sites are constantly created, the recently launched SimplyMarry.com, "India's only metro-monial site", for example, which addresses mainly an urban clientele. Furthermore, there are many websites which cater to specific communities or customers: Sikhingyou.com for Sikhs, Nikah.com for, Trinitymatrimony for Keralite Christians, are some examples. I have come across several Gujarati websites such as glagna.com and some which even specialize in distinct castes such as the Patels[5], Kutchi Lohanas[6] or BrahmKshatriya Sorathiya Vaishnavs.[7] The number of websites designed for an exclusive audience is growing steadily.

In 2007, the creators of Shaadi.com bridged another gap in the market by launching the website SecondShaadi.com, which is promoted as the "No.1 Re-marriage site for Indians". The site now operates independently from its mother-site Shaadi.com. By creating a marriage market for seekers of a second marriage, i.e. for divorcees and widowed people, the founders broke with traditional resentments since re-marriage, at least for traditional Hindus, has long been a taboo and is still not accepted all over the subcontinent. Even the

---

3   Most users are located in Mumbai (17%), followed by Delhi with 16%, Chennai, Kolkata and Bangalore (5-6%). See: IAMAI's Report on Matrimonial Search '2006':3-4.
4   Shaadi (Hindi): Marriage; Bharat (Hindi): India; Jeevansathi (Hindi): Life Partner.
5   www.patelvivah.com.
6   www.kutchilohana.com.
7   http://shaadi.brahmakshatriya.com.

general matrimonial sites contain the profiles of a significant percentage of widowed and divorced seekers, although the overwhelming majority of users has never been married (IAMAI's Report on Matrimonial Search '2006': 3).

Transnational Dynamics

Talking of the "Indian online matrimonial market" automatically covers more than the Indian subcontinent and refers to processes of de-territorialization. The translocal aspect inherent in the Internet holds great importance for online matrimonials. But at the same time, processes of reterritorialisation take place (Schneider and Gräf, 2010) and Hepp's approach of media as moulding forces thus needs to be expanded (see introduction to this volume). Media transgress territorial boundaries but as the example of the Indian diaspora shows, also cause a return to territory as identification point. Furthermore, the Indian matrimonial market reveals strong medial trends of regionalisation and localisation within India.[8]

Although, at the beginning of the "online boom" most users, especially NRIs from the United States, the United Kingdom, and the Gulf region[9], came from outside India, this ratio has undergone a huge change. At the moment about 70 percent of users come from India itself. They are either searching for a suitable partner within their respective diaspora community or looking for Indian candidates from the subcontinent itself. This implicates also a growing medialisation in India which goes beyond the cosmopolitan metros to small town contexts too. At the same time, the interaction of users in India with potential partners abroad is also increasing. The online matrimonial market is expanding as an Indian phenomenon but is not tied to a specific territory. Globally accessible matrimonial websites serve the Indian diaspora all over the world and provide it with the opportunity to connect with a transnational 'Indian' media and marriage market. To be Indian or "marry the Indian way", one doesn't need to live in India or hold Indian citizenship. The Indian diaspora's medial and thus social integration involves an advancing dissociation of 'nation' from 'territory'. The online matrimonial market helps thus to promote something which can be termed as "Global Indianness" because this market is

---

8   These trends are discussed in the conclusion.
9   Interview with shaadi.com PR Manager Gunjan Sinha, 16.4.2008.

simultaneously a global as well as national media product. Through this kind of medial integration the concept of 'national' or 'Indianness' is being "transnationalised" itself (Schneider, 2005: 76).

Localization of Global Influences: "The New Indian Woman"

Parallel to India's inclusion into a global media landscape, a nationalization or localization of global media influences can be observed (Fernandes, 2000). This is exemplified by the online matrimonial market. The design of India-based matrimonial websites includes patterns of traditional Indian matchmaking methods and requirements – so the Western idea of dating websites has been taken, transformed and adapted to the specific cultural context of India. This tendency has been termed as "nationalizing the global" by Leela Fernandes (Fernandes, 2000) and has an impact on medial representations of feminity as well. Media producers are well aware of changing perceptions. Advertisement, film and television makers have actively appropriated the trend in view of the increasing profits: "They have consequently begun to enlarge the range of feminine subjectivities which will increase consumption"(Munshi, 2001: 81). A "New Indian Woman" who pursues a global lifestyle but sticks to "Indian values" (Munshi, 2001; Fernandes, 2000; Rajan, 1993) has been constructed and mediated by the media since the 1980s (Mankekar, 1999 and 2009; Schneider, 2005: 52). The aspiring urban middle and upper classes, where this image is being located, constitute the online matrimonials' prime target group. The marriage market's influence is even further extended by the wedding industry which creates desire, distinction and status, and specialises in the marketing of style and etiquette, argues Brosius. Writing about India's urban middle class, she foregrounds weddings "as a stage for the display of 'world-class' lifestyle [...] and as they are imagined and communicated by lifestyle experts such as wedding planners." (Brosius, 2010: 276). New concepts are then transported far beyond urban centres due to the contemporary changes in India's media landscape towards localization and linguistic differentiation. Thus the image of the "New Indian Woman" is "shining" beyond the middle and upper classes, generating desire and longing in other segments of Indian society as well. The online matrimonial market is also influenced by medial constructions of femininity. Portraits of successful users and their stories are published by almost all websites as part of promotion strategies for proving their efficiency. Even a simple sentence such as "we chatted and spoke on the phone for hours" (Shaadi.com: Urdu Matrimonials[10]) alongside the photo of a female users carries a concept and intimates that communicating and getting to know each other is important when choosing a partner. Moreover, the fact that this statement is assigned to a woman implicates her agency in the process. Mass media products such as matrimonial websites are continuously permeated by such advertising messages, thus defining what is perceived as the norm and as a desirable existence (Dörner, 2001: 42). They are thus a striking example for a comprehensive development towards a society whose medial imprint is increasingly large.

Social Change: Self-Arranged Marriages

Even today, 90 percent of all marriages in India can be termed as "arranged". But the term's construction in opposition to the category of „love marriage" implies a simplified polarisation which cannot mirror actual social change. "We chatted for months and decided to go ahead before his parents spoke to my father" says "Sweta Jhoshi's story", another "True Story" advertised by Shaadi.com.[11] This leads to Kishwar's concept of "self-arranged marriage" instead of the fixed dualistic categories of love versus arrangement (Kishwar, 1994: 12). This example demonstrates the necessity of rethinking supposedly fixed categories to make processes of social change visible even within seemingly traditional concepts such as arranged marriage. A first impression might suggest that traditional patterns are perpetuated through the design and set-up of matrimonial websites. But examples derived from my case study in Mumbai 2008[12] reveal a considerably more complex picture: A survey conducted by Shaadi.com on the topic "What women want" included the question "After your marriage how would you like to live?", which was answered by 59, 6 percent of the respondents with "does not matter as long as you love your spouse" (Mehta, 2008).

---

10 http://ww2.shaadi.com/matrimonials/urdu-matrimonial (Accessed 20 October 2009). This particular image is not online anymore.
11 Retrieved from http://www.shaadi.com/introduction/true-stories.php
12 The case study consisted of 10 qualitative guided interviews with users of matrimonial websites. All names have been changed.

It shows clearly how significant the term "love" is even in an arranged marriage context. For most of my interview partners the term "love marriage" had a positive connotation and for many, an arranged marriage would have been the second choice: "A person who is not able to make it to a love marriage then he can go for arranged marriage, but if you are able to find someone on your own – nothing like it" (Arun).

The Internet offers the positive aspects of arranged marriages by enabling a systematic and selected search for specific criteria. These criteria, described as "equalizers" by an interview partner, maximize the chance of high compatibility regarding cultural and socio-economic background. Sharangpani observed similar patterns in matchmaking through marriage bureaus in Mumbai (Sharangpani, 2010). The major difference with regard to conventionally arranged marriages would be that many of these marriages are arranged by the individuals themselves. And this points once again to Kishwar's definition. She replaces the term "love marriage" with "self-arranged" and therewith differentiates between the family and the individual as agents (Kishwar, 1994: 12).

The divergent views on the classification of an "online match" reveal that the distinction between what is commonly called a love marriage and an arranged scenario is not at all clearly defined. On the one hand, the set-up is based on traditional categories such as 'religion', 'caste' and 'horoscope' thus resembling an arranged channel. This approach is definitely geared to conventional methods. On the other hand, websites such as Shaadi.com are also used simply as platforms or "meeting channels" for meeting new people, like in a chat room for example.

"Matrimonial site is just another avenue to get to know people, I wouldn't qualify it as arranged or love" (Anjali).

„Internet just became a medium for us to meet once and after that for months we just kept meeting, dating", one interviewee described the role of the Internet in regard to the relationship with his future wife. In contrast we also find marriages which have been arranged by the respective families in the conventional way, after the bride and groom's profiles were matched via a matrimonial website. Nevertheless, the medium offers the possibility of more individual initiative because websites often lie beyond the control of family networks.

The interviews verify the impression that the term "love marriage" employed by the interviewees resembled in many ways Kishwar's distinction between self- and family-arranged marriages: "I hold high regards for love marriage because you have an option of knowing the person before you marry" (Hema). A love marriage for Hema is a relationship where the partners get to know each other beforehand. "I think website marriages are like love marriages itself because it's not families that meet first, it's people that meet first" (Hema). In Hema's interpretation, love marriage is interrelated with individual initiative and agency and thus represents an opposite to a family-arranged scenario. Other interviewees emphasized that matrimonial websites can only lead to an arranged marriage because you register with an intention and not to meet a future partner occasionally.

How online-initiated marriages finally get settled depends strongly on the respective individuals and their families and the particular ways in which the medium is used. The Internet itself does not imply modernity and it does not have any intrinsic value system (see also Holst in this volume). It can be used for traditional purposes like a conventional family-arranged marriage but it also allows individual activities that go beyond the known patterns. Whether the result is described as arranged, love or "arranged cum love"[13] by the involved persons depends, on the one hand, on the subsequent procedure following the initial contact and, on the other, on the individual interpretation regarding the categories. An interviewee's attempt to describe her own marriage process within these categories illustrates how simplified the polarisation of love against pragmatic considerations is and that the dividing line is rather vague: „It was love because when we met we liked each other but it was arranged by us. So arranged cum love!" (Renuka). "Arranged" in this context implies that the couple has sought their parents' approval and assistance in the actual marriage organisation.

Changing Partner Preferences: Balancing Individual and Familial Orientation

All matrimonial websites contain, on top of the basic information on socio-religious background, for example, space for describing one's expectations and

---

13 Usually the term "arranged-cum-love" is used to describe a "love marriage" which is approved by the parents and thus socially legitimized.

partner preferences. Users are asked to write in their own words and to describe what they are looking for. These texts and the fields "About Me" (or "About Him/Her" if the profile was created by another person) are highly interesting sources for the analysis of current changes regarding the self-perception as well as future expectations of young women and men in contemporary Indian society. Thus "expectations and desired qualities" is an integral part of my research.

Media producers and market researchers are always keen to localize new trends and appropriate them for their own purposes. As already mentioned, Shaadi.com conducted a survey among 812 female users in 400 cities and towns across India between February and March 2008. The respondents were asked about the desired qualities of a future husband, their opinion on age differences, pre-marital sex, the organisation of their wedding, expectations about married life and many other points (Mehta, 2008). The study showed that compassion and understanding counted among a husband's essential qualities, followed by money and power. The salary had a high priority amongst the surveyed women with nearly half of them declaring they would not marry a man who earned less than themselves (Mehta, 2008). Vibhas Mehta, business head of Shaadi.com, also perceives the husband's profession as a deciding factor (Acharya, 2007: 13) because of its impact on financial stability in the household (Choudhury and Choudhury and Mohanty, 1995: 354). Three of the female users I have interviewed in Mumbai mentioned a solid financial status as the most decisive criterion for partner selection. This is further extended by the explicit emphasis of education which has been identified by Shukla and Kapadia's study and was confirmed in eight out of ten conducted interviews. Moreover, the interviews point out a noticeable interrelation between education and social status: "There are […] factors like education […] because you need to be at a certain level to maintain your social status"(Bhavna).

Shukla and Kapadia categorize relevant selection criteria according to two aspects:
- a) familial criteria such as religion, caste and family background and
- b) individual criteria such as character, looks and personality (Shukla and Kapadia, 2007: 42).

Their analysis of matrimonial advertisements in newspapers revealed a division of work between the family who is responsible for the scanning of familial criteria and the individual that is deciding over personal criteria (Shukla and

Kapadia, 2007: 47). The same pattern appeared in some of the interviews: "Parents try to analyze the family background whereas the person who is going to get married tries to analyze the would-be better half" (Arun).

Overall, personal criteria, particularly the character of the future "mate", seem to gain importance while familial criteria are gradually losing significance. Although certain qualities and talents have always been important, personality as a criterion is undergoing a very evident change. Notions such as integrity, loyalty, sense of humour and reliability appeared repeatedly during the interviews as well as in the analyzed website profiles. Many users look for someone they can talk to and who is a friend apart from being their spouse. Two individuals matching according to social markers and community membership do not necessarily make a good couple anymore. The concept of being personally compatible is gaining significance:

„I need someone to basically match more on the spiritual and emotional level and of course the physical. And if we are not connecting there, we probably will not get along very well" (Nitin).

Compatibility with the potential partner and his/her family is a notion which is of growing importance though this may encompass various aspects: compatibility according to professional qualifications, compatibility with the new family and their culture, compatibility of character, socio-economic compatibility, etc. In short, "Compatibility is the new buzzword"[14], as the Indian daily newspaper DNA has put it. Interpretations are shaped very individually. One interview partner regarded financial and educational background as an "equalizing" factor which could secure compatibility to a certain extent. Apart from economic aspects, the overall picture suggests a decrease in significance of traditional or familial criteria. Although the majority of interviewees asked for someone from the same religion, caste status played only a secondary or no role at all. In one case, religion was a factor, which was only considered for the parents' sake. Another woman said her mentioning of religion and caste was primarily intended to reduce the number of candidates. Astrology seems to be losing even more importance. None of the interview partners ascribed any kind of relevance to this criterion, so it seems to be another factor which is more important for the parental generation.

---

14 DNA Mumbai, 19.11.2007, p.13.

A preliminary conclusion could thus be that today's young generation assesses personal characteristics, education and career-oriented traits much more than the family background, which was considered the crucial factor for many centuries (Majumdar, 2004: 923). And accordingly, that the more the individual gets involved in the process of partner selection, the more familial criteria seem to lose significance whereas other categories come to the fore.[15] But the information derived from online matrimonial profiles showed remarkable differences. Almost half of the analyzed female profiles and more than a third of the male ones contained detailed information on the preferred caste membership of a partner. Regarding the female users this could be attributed to the active participation of other family members in the search process (more than 50% of the female profiles were created by others than the prospective bride). The proportion was comparatively lower among the male users. However, we cannot be sure whether the users would have explicitly emphasized caste as a relevant criterion if asked personally or whether it is employed simply as a limitation factor.

Overall, an area of conflict between individual wishes and familial expectations has become very obvious. Tensions were expressed during the interviews in particular but could be found in the analyzed website profiles as well. Within the Indian context, it seems that this tension doesn't necessarily cause a breach or conflict with the parental generation. "The youth also indicate a desire to exercise their choice but in consultation with parents or elders at home" (Rao and Rao, 1990:183). Family structures are still so fundamentally important that even when decisions are taken independently, any familial resistance is being avoided if somehow possible. "In a larger picture, I wouldn't upset my parents", emphasized 31 year old Bhavna during the interview. Shukla and Kapadia state as well that the marriage partner selection process shows glimpses of an "individualistic" orientation in a predominantly "collectivist" culture (Shukla and Kapadia, 2007: 48). This tendency shows the attempt to combine familial expectations and personal criteria. "It reflects a blending of individual related characteristics with efforts to incorporate the 'say' of the family" (ibid: 50). Instead, the attempt to balance individual and familial orientation possibly leads to inner conflicts for the individual. "The innate desire for conformity to the cultural ethos and the impact of the

---

15 A survey among Indian students about preferred future partners showed similar trends already in 1982 (See: Rao and Rao, 1990: 190).

changes often result in a chaotic situation" (ibid: 52). India's young urban generation is thus faced with the challenge of building bridges between them and the older generation.

Conclusion

In conclusion, I would like to point out that the evolution of the Indian online matrimonial market is occurring parallel to the general trends in Indian media development like regionalization and localization[16], for example. BharatMatrimony.com was the first online matrimonial service to realise the relevance of regional and local identification. Today, 15 regional sub-sites operate very successfully under the umbrella of BharatMatrimony.com. Furthermore, new regional websites such as Glagna.com ("For Gujaratis, By Gujaratis") or the Bengali daily *Anandabazar Patrika*'s matrimonial website Abppatropatri.com which offers "Bengali Matchmaking" are increasingly assertive on the market. The latter is an example of another highly interesting trend: the growing intermediality and media convergence. The involvement of print media such as *Anandabazar Patrika* or the *Times of India*, which is meanwhile cooperating with the matrimonial website SimplyMarry.com, illustrates the vague line between new and old media formats and the emergence of new mixed forms (Schneider, 2005: Chap. 1). The *Times of India* is not only cooperating with SimplyMarry.com as an online medium but also organises regular events called "Swayamvaras"[17], i.e. meeting forums for prospective brides and grooms and their families. These "marriage fairs" are organised according to communities and their realization and promotion is facilitated through partnerships with regional language or local print media. In November 2009, the troika of the *Times of India*, SimplyMarry.com and *Navbharat Times* (Hindi daily) hosted a "Punjabi Swayamvara" in Delhi (Sanvadadata, 2009). And in January 2010 they hosted a "Brahmin Swayamvara" (Sanvadata, 2010a) and an "Aggarwal Swayamvara" in March (Sanvadata,

---

16 For regionalization and localization of Indian media see: Ninan, 2007; Jeffrey, 2000; Schneider, 2005: Chap. 2.
17 Swayamvara (Sanskrit) was a practice of choosing a husband from among a list of suitors, by a girl of marriageable age. *Swayam* in Sanskrit means *Self* and *Vara* means *choosing or wanting*. The practice is known through its reference in the Hindu epics, most famously the Mahabharata. Today the term is used to describe partner selection in general, not only by the girl or woman.

2010b). Subscribers of SimplyMarry.com got discounted entry tickets and *Navbharat Times* and the *Times of India* advertised the event, which was also covered in their print editions.

The increasing cooperation between print and online media can be similarly observed throughout the news sector. Almost all Indian dailies and magazines operate their own websites with content exceeding the print version. Both media formats refer to each other and thus generate a convergent mixed format (see Schneider, 2005).

Finally, India's "Mobile Phone Revolution" also has an impact on the online matrimonial market. For instance, one can only validate a newly created profile on Shaadi.com by entering a mobile phone number. In addition, website features are not limited to browsing profiles but include chat, call and message modes, too. BharatMatrimony.com not only runs websites but also operates its own online TV channel, BharatMatrimony TV ("World's 1st Matrimony Channel") which features video polls on various questions (e.g. pre-marital courtship[18], love or arranged marriage[19], joint vs. nuclear family[20]), expert advice, success stories, etc. Herewith, matrimonial websites once more constitute a paradigmatic example for a general trend of media convergence and intermediality.

The intention of this article was to point out the interrelation of medialisation and social change by analysing the Indian online matrimonial market as an example and thus demonstrating the phenomenon's potential as a new field of research.

Based on the assumption of a fundamental connection between growing media acquisition and profound social change in contemporary Indian society, the online matrimonial market provides gateways to a multitude of highly relevant themes.

The interconnection between matrimonial advertisements and transnational dynamics in the context of migration and diaspora is having an effect on concepts of nation and "Indianness". The construction process of a modern Indian feminity also finds a medial platform to mediate and establish female ideals through advertisement and visual representation.

---

18 See http://tv.bharatmatrimony.com/video-polls/25-video-polls/493-pre-marital-courtship-1.
19 See http://tv.bharatmatrimony.com/video-polls/25-video-polls/88-love-or-arranged-marriage.
20 See http://tv.bharatmatrimony.com/video-polls/25-video-polls/97-joint-vs-nuclear-family.

The two case studies taken from my media analysis and field research demonstrate that social change can be made visible through the analysis of matrimonial websites and their users.

Despite the interrelation of media and social change, we have to be cautious not to follow single-tracked concepts of direct media impact as modernization theorists state. Media, in this case the Internet, are able to mirror and even influence socio-cultural change, but they can just as well perpetuate traditional patterns (Hepp, 2006: 40).

Bibliography

BANERJEE, A. V., 2009. *Marry for what? Caste and Mate Selection in Modern India.* Cambridge, Mass: National Bureau of Economic Research.

BERGMANN, J., 2006, Qualitative Methoden der Medienforschung. Einleitung und Rahmung. In: R. AYAß, ed. *Qualitative Methoden der Medienforschung.* Reinbek bei Hamburg: rororo, pp. 13–41.

BROSIUS, C., 2010. *India's Middle Class: New Forms of Urban Leisure, Consumption and Prosperity.* New Delhi: Routledge Chapman & Hall.

CHOUDHURY, B. & CHOUDHURY, R.K. & MOHANTY, S., 1995. Mate Selection Through Mass Media Aid, *Man in India*, 75 (4), pp. 339-354.

DÖRNER, A., 2001. *Politainment: Politik in der medialen Erlebnisgesellschaft.* Frankfurt am Main: Suhrkamp.

FERNANDES, L., 2000. Nationalizing the ‚Global': Media Images, Cultural Politics and the Middle Class in India, *Media, Culture and Society*, 22 (5), pp. 611-628.

HANKELN, M., 2008. *India's Marriages Re-Arranged: Changing Patterns Among the Urban Middle Class.* Saarbrücken: Vdm.

HEPP, A., 2006. *Transkulturelle Kommunikation.* Stuttgart: UTB.

HEPP, A., 2009. Transculturality as a Perspective. Researching Media Cultures Comparatively, *Forum: Qualitative Social Research*, 10 (1), [online] Available at: http://nbn-resolving.de/urn:nbn:de:0114-fqs0901267 [Accessed 10 May 2010].

HEPP, A., 2010. Mediatisierung und Kulturwandel: Kulturelle Kontextfelder und die Prägkräfte der Medien, In: M. HARTMANN & A. HEPP, eds. *Die Mediatisierung der Alltagswelt: Festschrift zu Ehren von Friedrich Krotz.* Wiesbaden: VS, pp. 65–84.

INTERNET & MOBILE ASSOCIATION OF INDIA (IAMAI), 2006. *IAMAI's Report on Matrimonial Search '2006'*, [online] Available at: http://www.iamai.in/Research.aspx?Fileid=r11_home.htm [Accessed 30 September 2010].

JEFFREY, R., 2000. *India's Newspaper Revolution: Capitalism, politics and the Indian-language press 1977-99.* London: Palgrave MacMillan.

JHA, S. & ADELMAN, M., 2009. Looking for Love in All the White Places: A Study of Skin Color Preferences on Indian Matrimonial and Mate-Seeking Websites. *Studies in South Asian Film and Media*, 1 (1), pp. 65-83.

KAUR, G., 2002. Marriages are Now a Mega Market. *Times of India*, 26 May, [online] Available at: http://timesofindia.indiatimes.com/articleshow/11007826.cms [Accessed 6 August 2008].

KIM, Y., ed., 2008. *Media Consumption and Everyday Life in Asia.* New York: Routledge Chapman & Hall.

KISHWAR, M., 1994. Love and Marriage, *Manushi*, (80), pp. 11-19.

MAJUMDAR, R., 2004. Looking for Brides and Grooms: Ghataks, Matrimonials and the Marriage Market in Bengal, c. 1875-1940, *Journal of Asian Studies*, 63 (4), pp. 911-935.

MANKEKAR, P., 1999. *Screening Culture, Viewing Politics: Ethnography of Television, Womanhood, and Nation in Postcolonial India*. Durham, N.C.: Duke University Press.

MANKEKAR, P., 2009. 'Women-Oriented' Narratives and the New Indian Woman, In: A. RAJAGOPAL, ed. *The Indian Public Sphere: Readings in Media History*. New Delhi: Oxford University Press, pp. 135-150.

MEHTA, Business Head of Shaadi.Com, in Conversation with Preety Acharya, *DNA (Daily News & Analysis)*, Mumbai, 19 November, p. 13.

MEHTA, N. T., 2008. What Women Want, *Hindustan Times*, 8 March.

MUNSHI, S., 2001. Marvellous Me: The Beauty Industry and the Construction of the 'Modern' Indian Woman, In: S. MUNSHI, ed. *Images of the 'Modern Woman' in Asia: Global Mdia, Local Meanings*. Richmond: RoutledgeCurzon, pp.78-93.

N.A., 2007. Compatibility is the New Buzzword, *DNA (Daily News & Analysis)*, Mumbai, 19 November, p. 13.

NINAN, S., 2007. *Headlines from the Heartland: Reinventing the Hindi public sphere*. Los Angeles: Sage.

PEPPER, D., 2007. Indische Heiratsportale: Per Mausklick zum Eheglück, *Spiegel online*, 15 April, [online] Available at: http://www.spiegel.de/netzwelt/web/0,1518,477062,00.html [Accessed 8 July 2008].

RAJAN, R., 1993. *Real and Imagined Women: Gender, Culture, and Postcolonialism*. London: Routledge Chapman & Hall.

RAO, V. N. & RAO, V. V. P., 1990. Desired Qualities in a Future Mate in India, *International Journal of Sociology of the Family*, (20), pp. 181-198.

SANVADADATA, V., 2009. Times Panjabi Svayamvar ne banaaii joriyan [Hindi], *Navbharat Times*, 30 November.

SANVADADATA, V., 2010a. Saathi kii talaash mein thand beiriyar nahin: SimplyMarry.com ke svayamvar mein ravivaar ko juuti bhaarii bhiir [Hindi], *Navbharat Times*, 18 January.

SANVADADATA, V., 2010b. To bat pakki: Svayamvar ne kii partner kii talaash aasaan: SimplyMarry.com ke program mein bhaarii bhiir, 550 shaamil aur website par 185 registration [Hindi], *Navbharat Times*, 15 March.

SCHNEIDER, N.-C., 2005. *Zur Darstellung von „Kultur" und „kultureller Differenz" im indischen Mediensystem: Die indische Presse und die Repräsentation des Islams im Rahmen der Zivilrechtsdebatte, 1985-87 und 2003*. Berlin: Logos.

SCHNEIDER, N.-C., 2007. Medienpluralismus in Indien. Fernsehen, Presse und Hörfunk entwickeln sich dynamisch, *Bundeszentrale für politische Bildung*, 27 January, [online] Available at: http://www.bpb.de/themen/IBDE4P,0,0,Medienpluralismus_in_Indien.html [Accessed 2 November 2010]

SCHNEIDER, N.-C. & GRÄF, B., 2010. Tagungsbericht Zeit für Medialisierung: Medien und transkulturelle Kommunikation in den Islam- und Regionalwissenschaften. 10.04.2010-12.04.2010, Berlin, *H-Soz-u-Kult*, 11 June, [online] Available at: http://hsozkult.geschichte.hu-berlin.de/tagungsberichte/id=3148 [Accessed 3 November 2010]

SETH, N. & PATNAYAKUNI, R., 2009. Online Matrimonial Sites and the Transformation of Arranged Marriage in India, In: C. ROMM-LIVERMORE, & K. SETZEKORN, ed., *Social Networking Communities and E-Dating Services: Concepts and Implications*. Hershey: Idea Group Publishing.

SHARANGPANI, M., 2010. Browsing for Bridegrooms: Matchmaking in Mumbai, *Indian Journal of Gender Studies*, 17(2), pp. 249-276.

SHARDA, B. D., 1990. Marriage Markets and Matrimonial Matchmaking Among Asian Indian of the United States, *International Journal of Sociology of the Family*, 20 (1), pp. 21-29.

SHARMA, A., 2008. Caste on Indian Marriage dot-com: Presence and Absence, In: R. Gajjala, ed. *South Asian Technospaces*. New York: Peter Lang, pp. 135-151.

SHUKLA, S. & KAPADIA, S., 2007. Transition in Marriage Partner Selection Process. Are Matrimonial Advertisements an Indication?, *Psychology & Developing Societies*, 19 (1), pp. 37-54.

Matrimonial Websites

www.abppatropatri.com
www.bharatmatrimony.com
www.glagna.com
www.indianmatrimonials.com
www.jeevansathi.com
www.kutchilohana.com
www.lifepartnerindia.com
www.matrisearch.com
www.merasathi.com
www.nikah.com
www.patelvivah.com
www.pyar.org
www.secondshaadi.com
www.shaadi.com
http://shaadi.brahmakshatriya.com
www.sikhingyou.com
www.simplymarry.com
www.trinitymatrimony.com

BharatMatrimonyTV:
http://tv.bharatmatrimony.com/ [Accessed 1 September 2010].
http://tv.bharatmatrimony.com/video-polls/25-video-polls/493-pre-marital-courtship-1
http://tv.bharatmatrimony.com/video-polls/25-video-polls/88-love-or-arranged-marriage
http://tv.bharatmatrimony.com/video-polls/25-video-polls/97-joint-vs-nuclear-family

CLAUDIA NEF SALUZ

Dakwahkampus.com as Informal Student Web Portal of Hizbut Tahrir Indonesia

Introduction

The Islamic scholar Taqiyyudin An-Nabhani (1909–1977) founded Hizbut Tahrir (Party of Liberation)[1] in Jerusalem in 1952.[2] Hizbut Tahrir is currently active in over forty-five countries (Osman, 2009: 1). In Indonesia, Hizbut Tahrir may be seen as the organisation that most prominently demands the establishment of a global caliphate *(khilafah)* and the implementation of the *Sharia*. Compared with the two large-scale Muslim organizations Nahdlatul Ulama and Muhammadiyah, which together represent more than 75 million of Indonesia's 200 million Muslims (Bush, 2009: 2), the organisation could be seen as rather marginal. However, the agenda of Hizbut Tahrir finds support in these much larger organisations, which do not have the implementation of the *Sharia* on their agendas (Schulze 2008: 40). Since the ideology of Hizbut Tahrir reached Indonesia in 1982, it has mainly found support among students and well-educated professionals in Indonesia's urban centres. (Osman, 2009: 11; Fealy, 2007: 156; Muhtadi, 2009: 629). In 2000, the organisation made its public appearance when it held its first International Caliphate Conference in Jakarta, attended by around five thousand activists (Osman, 2009: 7). In the past decades, Hizbut Tahrir Indonesia has increased its membership and general support considerably, and by 2007, more than 100'000 people attended the International Caliphate Conference in Jakarta (Ward, 2009: 625).

---

1 Hizbut Tahrir calls itself a party *(hizb)*, and at times even a political party. The founder of the organisation, An-Nabhani, saw it as the religious obligation *(fard)* of Muslims to establish an Islamic party in order to construct an Islamic state. He states that Muhammad Himself called his group a party. For a detailed discussion of the term, see Taji-Farouki (1996: 84-5). As Hizbut Tahrir is, however, not involved in party politics, I will use the term organisation.

2 For arguably the most comprehensive account of the early history of Hizbut Tahrir, see Taji-Farouki 1996.

In the years after founding Hizbut Tahrir, An-Nabhani developed in his numerous writings an ideology *(mabda')* that he considered applicable to everyday life. This ideology offered solutions to individual problems as well as guidelines for regulating and ordering societal and public affairs. For An-Nabhani, Islam provides a complete blueprint for a distinctively Islamic government whose form has been divinely prescribed in the Koran and in the sayings and deeds of the prophet Muhammad *(hadith)* As such, he considered it self-evident that the state is an intrinsic part of Islam (Taji-Farouki, 1996: 64). In his writings he sought to provide an alternative to socialism and capitalism, as he considered both of these secular ideologies responsible for the decline of the Muslim world (ibid: 39).

As mainly students and well-educated professionals support the organisation, media usage is crucial both for internal and external communication. The four most comprehensive studies of Hizbut Tahrir Indonesia in recent years show that the organisation is adept at using both traditional and new media technology (Osman, 2009; Muhtadi, 2009; Ward, 2009; Fealy, 2007). The group has long committed to producing a wide range of printed media. The organisation has its own publishing houses, *Pustaka Thariqul Izzah* and *Al-Izzah* Press (Osman, 2009: 13; Fealy, 2007: 155-6). In 2006, Hizbut Tahrir Indonesia opened HTI press, which focuses on translating Hizbut Tahrir books into Indonesian (Osman, 2009: 13). Other publishing houses affiliated with Hizbut Tahrir Indonesia are *Al-Kautsar* Press, *Khilafah* Press, PTI and WADI Press. These houses mainly publish books written by Indonesian Hizbut Tahrir activists, who relate the organisation's ideology to contemporary issues.[3] The published books are meant for mass circulation and can be purchased online or in usually small, specific bookstores, which Hizbut Tahrir activists often run. Since 1993, Hizbut Tahrir Indonesia has also published the weekly bulletin *Al-Islam*, which is freely distributed at Friday prayers each week. *Al-Waïe*, a monthly journal published since 2000 (Osman, 2009: 14), relates the ideology of the organisation to contemporary problems in a more sophisticated manner than this is done in the bulletin *Al-Islam*, which is addressed to a larger public.[4]

---

[3] See http://pasarkhilafah.com/, [Accessed 18 August 2010], for an extensive overview of currently available books in Indonesia.

[4] See Schulze (2008) for a content analysis of *Al-Waïe* regarding Hizbut Tahrir's views on pluralism and democracy. Past editions of *Al-Waïe* can be accessed on the official website of Hizbut Tahrir Indonesia http://hizbut-tahrir.or.id.

Hizbut Tahrir also uses online resources to disseminate its ideas, most prominently through its official website, http://hizbut-tahrir.or.id. This site features a wealth of information presented in formats that range from articles on various topics and photos to videos. A professional team produces the majority of the videos. They are responsible for documenting different events such as conferences, workshops and demonstrations (Osman 2009: 14). Videos of Hizbut Tahrir, both more and less professionally produced ones, can also be accessed on video-sharing websites such as YouTube.[5]

Even though Osman briefly points to the fact that many Hizbut Tahrir members also use informal Internet platforms that are not officially linked to the organisation (2009: 15), he does not elaborate on how such activities might look or what opportunities and challenges the Internet might provide for students. Similarly, Fealy, Muhtadi, and Ward do not ask how new technologies such as the Internet may not only influence strategies for disseminating ideas, but also open up new ways for a larger group of young Hizbut Tahrir members to address a wider public. To address this research gap, this article examines the web portal *Dakwahkampus.com*, or *DK.com* in short, which is not officially linked to Hizbut Tahrir, but nevertheless mirrors its ideology.

By taking *DK.com* as an example, I argue that media effects must not be understood in terms of a polarity between what are often assumed to be two contradictory processes: on the one hand is the disciplinary effect of media, in which media are a vehicle for carrying ideologies to a passive citizenry, and on the other hand is the deliberative character of media, in which media offer a democratic opportunity to foster argumentation and dialogue.[6] Baran, for example, states that, "It (Hizbut Tahrir) indoctrinates individuals with radical ideology" (2005: 68). Ali's analysis goes in the same direction, as he notes that innocent youth are driven into the hands of fundamentalists such as Hizbut Tahrir as a result of being indoctrinated through media (Ali, 2006: 61). Studies stressing the disciplinary effects of media ground their analyses in the perception that media technologies enable the extension of an authoritative religious

---

5   See http://www.youtube.com/results?search_query=hizbut+tahrir+indonesia&aq=f, [Accessed 18 August 2010], for examples.
6   In his research on the role of cassette sermons in contemporary Cairo, Hirschkind (2001, 2006) has most prominently argued against this dualistic perception of media effects.

discourse. In this case, the resultant public is less a sphere of discussion than a site of subjection to authority. This is seen as part of an endeavour to promote and secure a uniform model of moral behaviour among followers. I will however argue that given the social reality of student activists on campuses where different Islamic groups seek to promote their own understandings of Islam, it is indispensable to assume a contested public sphere where activists are not simply "indoctrinated" but rather engage in regular discussion with peers. I therefore argue that both disciplinary and deliberative media effects are inextricably interwoven in the everyday lives of Islamic student activists.

I begin this article by introducing the reader to the web portal *DK.com* and exploring how it is linked to Hizbut Tahrir as an avenue for informal communication. I then discuss an article written by a prominent member of Hizbut Tahrir posted on the portal to underline my argument that disciplinary and deliberative media effects are entangled. Before concluding, I reflect on how people alter their ways of knowledge dissemination and mobilization strategies when using the Internet. The analysis of *DK.com* is embedded into insights gained during almost two years of anthropological fieldwork conducted at Gadjah Mada University in Yogyakarta about contemporary forms of Islamic student activism in 2005-06 and 2008-09.

The Web Portal *Dakwahkampus.com*

The web portal *Dakwahkampus.com* was founded in 2009 by student activists of different University Dakwah Organisations (LDK)[7] with the aim of coordinating information, intellectual discussions and movement strategies among different student *dakwah* activists. It currently registers around 1'000 daily visits.[8] *DK.com* defines itself as the online communication organ of the Coor-

---

7   Most Indonesian universities have an LDK, or *Lembaga Dakwah Kampus*, that is in charge of taking care of the needs and demands of Muslim students. Groups often receive both limited funding and office space from the universities with which they are affiliated. The majority of University Dakwah Organisations were founded in the 1980s and early 1990s (Sidiq, 2003: 72). Currently, Hizbut Tahrir and *tarbiyah* activists dominate most LDKs of the major secular Indonesian universities. In addition to a variety of Islamic organisations, many non-Islamic student organisations also exist.

8   For the current number of daily, weekly and monthly visits, see http://dakwah kampus.com/, [Accessed 23 August 2010].

dinating Body of University Dakwah Organisations (BKLDK), which was founded in Bogor five years earlier by *dakwah* activists from different Indonesian Universities.[9] The portal is mainly designed to address students. In the profile of *DK.com*, students are described as important agents of social change. It is assumed that they will become future leaders of the country and of the Muslim community, as their intellectual capacity is above average. They will thus be in positions of authority in the struggle to encourage fellow students to become "better Muslims".[10]

DK.com is not explicitly linked to Hizbut Tahrir Indonesia; indeed the organisation is rarely mentioned on the portal. Rather than addressing Hizbut Tahrir members or even sympathizers, the authors seek to speak to *dakwah* activists in general. The term *dakwah* (arab. *da'wa*), as found in the name of the web portal, has historically encompassed a broad range of meanings; literally, it may be translated as "summon" or "call". In the Indonesian context, as well as in other parts of the world, *dakwah* is commonly understood as the "duty, incumbent upon some or all members of the Islamic community, to actively encourage fellow Muslims in the pursuance of greater piety in all aspects of their lives" (Hirschkind, 2006: 108-9). The most cited Koranic reference for this interpretation is verse 3:104: "And that there might grow out of you a community (of people) who invite unto all that is good, and enjoin the doing of what is right and forbid the doing of what is wrong: as it is they, they who shall attain to a happy state".[11]

The ideological orientation of the portal, which I outline below, is not explicitly related to Hizbut Tahrir or to the writings of An-Nabhami. However, its ideological affiliation manifests itself in a variety of ways. In addition to more and less well-known campus activists, many high-ranking Hizbut Tahrir members also contribute articles, even as they do so without exerting authority

---

9   For a detailed profile of the BKLDK (*Badan Koordinasi Lembaga Dakwah Kampus*) see http://dakwahkampus.com/profil/bkldk.html, [Accessed 19 August 2010]. This coordinating body is only one of many organisations aiming to coordinate activities of different University Dakwah Organisations. Bigger and better known is the Friendship Forum of University Dakwah Organisations, founded in 1986 in Yogyakarta, which reflects the ideology of the *tarbiyah* movement. (Sidiq, 2003: 75).
10 For a detailed profile of DK.com see http://dakwahkampus.com/profil/dakwah kampuscom.html, [Accessed 1 September 2010].
11 Translated by Asad (2003). Other verses often cited for emphasising the duty to call others to Islam are 3:110 and 16:125.

by mentioning their positions within the organisation, as is otherwise typically done in official Hizbut Tahrir media releases. Besides the obvious ideological affiliation, the logo of Hizbut Tahrir[12] is highly visible on numerous photos and on videos that can be downloaded from the portal. Numerous cross references to events promoted on the portal can also be found on the official webpage of Hizbut Tahrir Indonesia. While the reasons for not explicitly linking the organisation to the portal might be many and varied, one significant effect is that it allows the portal to address a broader public of different *dakwah* activists.

On the web portal interested readers can access texts arranged in different rubrics:
  I. news: divided in "news of the Islamic world", "prime focus", primarily focusing on national news, and "news from the campus";
  II. consultation: including the categories "question and answer for female students", "consultation concerning *dakwah* activities on the campus" and "*Ustadz* (Islamic teacher) responds";
  III. articles: embracing the categories "student's opinions", "ideology", "female students" and "personality";
  IV. organisational profiles: including the one of *DK.com* and the coordinating body BKLDK.

In addition to the text files, videos and photos from different demonstrations and workshops can also be accessed. One of the most-opened files on the portal is a technically well-made video of the first Indonesian Islamic Student Congress *(Kongres Mahasiswa Islam Indonesia)*, which was held in Jakarta on October 18, 2009. The congress was organised by the BKLDK and promoted on *DK.com*. In the introduction, an anonymous male speaker describes the congress as:

… a moment in history, that was attended by thousands of students from all Indonesia, the greatest moment in the history of Islamic student

---

12 The logo of Hizbut Tahrir, the white and black flag (*liwa* and *rayah*) could theoretically also be used by other Islamic groups, as Hizbut Tahrir activists claim that they were used by the Prophet. In Indonesia, these two flags with the inscription, "There is no God except Allah and Mohammed is his messenger," are however commonly identified as logo of Hizbut Tahrir (see Budiarti, 2009). The flags are also omnipresent on the webpage of Hizbut Tahrir as well as on the different publications.

movement that unites and creates an intellectual student vision to make Indonesia a better place, a new direction in the student movement, a pledge will be born.[13]

This whole introduction is underlined by sound, creating a mood of anticipation. One can then listen to extracts of the speeches delivered by three prominent Hizbut Tahrir members, namely Fahmi Amhar, Dwi Condro Triono and Fahmi Lukman, who seek to raise awareness of problems Indonesia faces in the fields of natural resource management, economy, and education, respectively. They address the more than 5'000 students who convened in the yard outside Senayan Basket Hall, as the police had not allowed students to hold the event inside the hall as they had originally planned. The students Felix Siauw, Pariadi Hartono and Adi Wijaya also delivered speeches emphasising that "Islam is the only solution" and motivating the crowd to struggle for the achievement of this ultimate goal through *dakwah*. The enthusiastic audience often chanted "Caliphate!" Repeatedly the speakers shouted "*takbir*," and the crowd responded with a chorus of "*Allahu Akbar*" (God is greater), raising their right fists.

The dramaturgical culmination of the video as well as the most important part of the congress was the reading out loud of the Student's Pledge *(Sumpah Mahasiswa)*. This pledge mirrors the ideology of Hizbut Tahrir in a nutshell. It can be downloaded in different forms from *Dakwahkampus.com*, in text, photos or audio. At the congress, the national coordinator of the BKLDK, Erwin El-Jundi, read the pledge, stopping every few words to permit the audience to repeat:

1. With all our soul, we believe that secular systems – either capitalist democratic or socialist communist – are sources of people's deprivation and endanger the existence of Indonesia and other Muslims countries.
2. With all our heart, we believe that absolute sovereignty is reserved solely to Allah – the creator of the universe, humanity and life – to decide the future of Indonesia and other Muslim countries.

---

13 The video can be downloaded from http://dakwahkampus.com/berita/isu-utama/189.html, [Accessed 19 August 2010].

3. With all our soul, we will continue to relentlessly fight for the enactment of the *Sharia* under the caliphate as the ultimate solution to the problems of Indonesia and other Muslim societies.
4. With our soul, we declare to all that our struggle is verbal and intellectual, and not violent.
5. With our soul, we declare that our struggle is not a consequence of historical demands, but is instead a consequence of deep faith to Allah.[14]

In the aftermath of the Jakarta congress, student activists read out the same pledge in different Indonesian cities, organising similar congresses, workshops or public events. The happenings were announced on *DK.com*, which then posted photos and reports after the events. As *DK.com* is on Facebook[15], the events were also announced and discussed on this social networking website.

DK.com is hierarchically structured, with a head of redaction, a head of administration and staff responsible for handling contributions from local partners. The web portal is thus not an open space where anyone can upload documents, photos or videos. No articles can be found that are out of line with the ideology of the administrators as stated in the pledge. Contributions have to pass through the editorial team before being put online. All authors are asked to provide their full identities, and no opportunities for anonymous "comments" exist. It is, however, possible for anyone to comment on articles on Facebook. Critical comments – for example, those that question whether the caliphate is an ultimate solution – are rare, as people who join this group tend to sympathise with its general ideology.

---

14 My own translation. For the Indonesian version and further description of the pledge, see http://dakwahkampus.com/artikel/pemikiran/136.html, [Accessed 19 August 2010].
15 Facebook is an online social networking site launched in 2004, where people and organisations can create profiles to inform others about themselves or about the organisation. Users have than the chance to join networks or fan communities initiated by different individuals regarding a vast number of topics. Communication between different users may be done through sending private or public messages. See www.facebook.com.

Entangled Disciplinary and Deliberative Media Effects

By taking one article posted on *DK.com* as an example I wish to emphasise that the effects of *DK.com* can not be fully understood in terms of the indoctrination of passive individuals. As different articles on the portal show, the activists face a variety of problems when it comes to convincing fellow students to change their attitudes and beliefs. By examining an article posted on *DK.com* in March 2010 by Zamroni Ahmad, a member of the Central Executive Board of Hizbut Tahrir Indonesia *(Dewan Pimpinan Pusat)*, I show how the public arena is used as a deliberative space for argumentation among different individuals and, *at the same time,* as a normative space for promotion of individuals' own visions of Islamic virtue (Hirschkind, 2001, 2006).

In research on the role of new media technology in constituting Islamic activism, scholars have *either* stressed the disciplinary *or* the deliberative effects of media (Hirschkind, 2001: 3). Examples of studies that highlight the disciplinary effects of modern media technology in the context of Islam in general are Roy (1996) and Sivan (1990), and in the context of Islam in Indonesia more specifically, Lim (2005) and Bräuchler (2003). Others have emphasised the deliberative effects of modern media technology in the Middle East in regard to the democratisation of religious authority and cultivation of autonomous reasoning facilitated by the growing number of individuals engaging with religious texts, including Eickelman (1992), Eickelman and Anderson (1997) and some of the contributors to the volume edited by Norton (1995). In Indonesia, Hosen (2008) identifies a democratisation of religious authority due to the increasing number of Muslims who choose to exercise choice in finding personally suitable Islamic legal opinions *(fatwas)* by searching different Islamic websites.

In the article I move on to discuss titled "Attitudes towards differences and frictions between student *dakwah* movements"[16], Zamroni Ahmad focuses on how to handle differences among various Islamic student movements on campus and then discusses strategies to convince other activists that they are

---

16 See http://dakwahkampus.com/konsultasi/konsultasi-dakwah-kampus/743-menyikapi-perbedaan-dan-pergesekan-antar-gerakan-dakwah-kampus.html/, [Accessed 8 March 2010].

interpreting the Koran and the *hadith* in an "incorrect" way. He does not explicitly address Hizbut Tahrir activists in his article, but rather talks about "ideological activists" *(aktivis ideologis)*. This allows him to address a potentially larger group than Hizbut Tahrir activists and sympathisers. He defines "ideological activists" in a narrow way as those activists who present clear-cut solutions to problems facing the Islamic community and who are systematic in their line of argumentation. Hizbut Tahrir activists often praise themselves as being most logical and stringent in their way of argumentation and most coherent in the ultimate solution they propose – the re-establishment of the caliphate. An-Nabhani himself also framed Hizbut Tahrir as the most rational, comprehensive movement (Taji-Farouki, 1996: 45-7).

Ahmad starts his article by cautioning *dakwah* activists against assuming that the process of convincing others will be smooth and problem-free. The text is than divided into two parts, in which Ahmad first discusses "internal" and then "external" factors that may cause friction among different Islamic activists. In the first part of the article he addresses the mentality a *dakwah* activist needs to have as a precondition to convincing others. She or he must be sure that the others must be "brought back to the straight path" and that they are objects of *dakwah (obyek dakwah)* rather than equal competitors. The types of outreach other Islamic groups are doing, he states, does thus not need to be seen as "real" *dakwah*, as these students are exploited by political parties who send out their socialist and liberal henchmen in Islamic dress at election time. He is not specific about which Islamic organisations he considers to be doing "fake" *dakwah*. With his statement about students exploited by political parties, he seems however to be implicitly referring, among others, to the adherents of the *tarbiyah* movement, which supports the Justice and Welfare Party (PKS) and draws its ideological inspiration from the Muslim Brothers[17]. It is thus in his opinion not tolerable to adopt a pluralistic view and let others practice Islam in the ways they think are correct. *Dakwah* activists, he claims, must fully understand that only they have truly understood the message of Allah.

---

17 See Taji-Farouki for a detailed account of the ideological differences between Hizbut Tahrir and the Muslim Brothers. One of the most significant differences is Hizbut Tahrir's rejection of gradualism as a way to reach the ultimate goal of establishing the Caliphate (1996: 111-112).

In the second part of the article, Ahmad discusses "external" factors that might lead to friction among different Islamic activists and make convincing others of what he sees as the "truth" difficult. He focuses in particular on the resistance of other Islamic activists to embracing the ideology of Hizbut Tahrir. To mitigate this friction and convince others, the "ideological activists" should follow a certain path: After they are certain that they are the authentic activists, they should visit the other active Islamic groups on campus one by one to explain their existence and mission clearly and understandably. All organizations should be invited to join the organized events. The "ideological activists" should furthermore try to work together with the different organizations whenever possible, but make sure that they are the leaders and main actors. They should always remind others that global capitalism is the common enemy and avoid making it seem as if they were the common enemy of other Islamic groups.

In addition to actively diagnosing problems and providing Islamic solutions, "ideological activists" should also always remember to behave in a morally Islamic manner and follow the ethical model of the Prophet. Ahmed suggests, for example, treating intellectuals of other Islamic movements with respect, taking care not to insult or humiliate them. He further suggests that "ideological activists" make the first steps in approaching other activists to congratulate them on major Islamic holy days, such as *Idul Fitri* (marking the end of Ramadan), *Idul Adaha* (feast of sacrifice) and the Islamic New Year. Furthermore, if "ideological activists" hear others complain about their behaviour, they should visit them and try to solve the problem through dialogue. Those who issued the complaints should be reminded that the enemies of Islam hope for internal quarrels among Islamic groups, as this will weaken the *ummat*, the worldwide Islamic community. In addition to these rationally based arguments[18], Ahmad also stresses the need to be emotionally sensitive. For example, he states that it is important to bring gifts, as Islam sees this as a favourable behaviour. "Ideological activists" should behave more maturely and not respond harshly or impolitely. They have to stay calm and maintain equanimity, behaving like a big sister or brother should behave towards his or her young sibling.

---

18 For a detailed account about the rationality of the ideology of Hizbut Tahrir, see Taji-Farouki (1996: 45-7).

Ahmad's article ascribes a salient role to debate and argumentation in the everyday activities of *dakwah* activists. Because *dakwah* is undertaken in public places with the aim of enforcing public virtue, some *dakwah* activities might be seen as an unwarranted intrusion into the personal privacy of those Muslims who tend to see virtue as a matter of private choice. Moral issues in particular, such as the modesty of one's dress, proximity of unrelated men and women, and consumption patterns, often become sites of confrontation and pose challenges to maintaining intra-religious tolerance. Whereas Hizbut Tahrir activists perceive these issues as crucial to establishing the caliphate and therefore not as matters of individual choice, others argue that they are secondary for "making Islam become a blessing to all" *(rahmatan lil alamin)*. At stake in these debates are different imaginations of personal and collective freedom. *Dakwah* activists thus constantly traverse the distinction between public and private. At least in some respect, their behaviour may be seen as deviant from secular-liberal expectations of critical reasoning.. The distinction between private and public is not fixed, but an issue of constant negotiation.

Engagement in Web Communities Versus Formal Membership

University Dakwah Organisations (LDK) have been playing an important role in disseminating the ideology of Hizbut Tahrir since the beginning, and the LDK of the Bogor Agricultural Institute in particular has become a stronghold of Hizbut Tahrir (Fealy, 2007: 156). It is thus not surprising that the coordinating body BKLDK was founded in Bogor. The BKLDK has however no legal authority over these University Dakwah Organisations, which may or may not choose to become members of the BKLDK or access services such as different kinds of trainings and workshops organised in different Indonesian cities and promoted also on *DK.com*.

DK.com is, however, more than the formal communication organ of the coordinating body BKLDK; it also has several characteristics of a distinct independent community. When, for example, events are organized, the logo of the *DK.com* community appears alongside the logo of the BKLDK. *DK.com*'s Facebook profile has almost 16'000 users who have claimed that they "like" the page. In addition to individuals, organizations and communities have also declared that they "like" *DK.com*, among them different local branches of the

Muhammadiyah Student Organisation IMM (*Ikatan Mahasiswa Muhammadiyah*), and local branches of the Justice and Welfare Party PKS (*Partai Keadilan Sejahtera*). The BKLDK, on the other hand, has a Facebook community only about a tenth of the size of *DK.com's*.[19] The strategic choice to appear as a relatively detached community has the advantage of potentially addressing all campus *dakwah* activists, rather than only the members of different University Dakwah Organisations. *DK.com* is thus more inclusive in character than the BKLDK.

In his study of Hizbut Tahrir's discourses on pluralism and democracy in Indonesia, Schulze shows that the organisation's ideology seems to find acceptance and even support among *mainstream* Islamic organisations such as Muhammadiyah (2008: 40). He also notes that the relations between the Justice and Welfare Party PKS and Hizbut Tahrir are cordial (ibid: 39). He bases his study, however, on the words and actions of high-ranking members, such as Din Syamsuddin who has been chairman of Muhammadiyah since 2005. From conducting interviews with different student activists of the Gadjah Mada University, I have observed that also on the grassroots level, the ideology of Hizbut Tahrir finds much broader support among a range of different student organisations, including HMI-MPO[20], IMM[21] as well as KAMMI[22]. Whereas in HMI-MPO some activists are official Hizbut Tahrir members, KAMMI, which is part of the *tarbiyah* movement, draws its ideological inspiration from the Muslim Brothers, which partly opposes Hizbut Tahrir's ideology.[23] It is nevertheless interesting to note that both organisations "like" *DK.com* and attend at least some discussions and promoted activities. On *DK.com*, a variety of topics are discussed that are also on the agendas of other organisations.

---

19 See http://www.facebook.com/felix.siauw#!/pages/Dakwah-kampus/209564192379 and http://id-id.facebook.com/group.php?gid=176100947877, [Accessed 17 August 2010].
20 Himpunan Mahasiswa Islam – Majelis Penyelamat Organisasi (*Muslim Student's Association – The Assembly of the Savers of the Organisation*)
21 Ikatan Mahasiswa Muhammadiyah (*Muhammadiyah Student Organisation*)
22 Kesatuan Aksi Mahasiswa Muslim Indonesia (*Indonesian Muslim Student Action Unit*)
23 For understanding the linkages between the *tarbiyah* movement more generally, KAMMI and the political Justice and Welfare Party PKS see Damanik (2002) and Sidiq (2003).

Due to the anonymity an individual enjoys while surfing the web portal, becoming familiar with the ideas of Hizbut Tahrir does not demand personal commitment; at this casual stage, it is not yet necessary to change one's behaviour. Expressing support for *DK.com*, for example by "liking" it on Facebook, technically only demands clicking a single button, whereas becoming a member of Hizbut Tahrir is a process that may take one or two years (Taji-Farouki, 1996: 133). The fluid and dynamic network of followers that emerges supersedes the moral and geographical boundaries of the Indonesian state and is thus more open and inclusive than the organisation whose ideology it reflects. A contributor or active participant need not have a vertical affiliation to any organisation as long as one's contributions conform to the group's ideology. Electronically mediated participation may thus be seen to be facilitating the emergence of new mobilization structures. Peer-to-peer communication allows creating schemata for diagnosing problems likely to resonate strongly with the needs of the target group – the students.

As opposed to *DK.com*'s fluid network of followers, Hizbut Tahrir maintains a three-level membership structure that demands different levels of commitment (Taji-Farouki, 1996: 114-152; Osman, 2009: 9). Before becoming a member, a novice has to follow the weekly meetings of the study circles *(halaqah)* and master at least three fundamental texts by An-Nabhani, including *Nizam al-Islam* (The System of Islam, 1953), in which the constitution for an Islamic state is outlined, *Mafahim Hizbut Tahrir* (Concepts of Hizbut Tahrir, 1953) and *al-Takattul al-Hizbi* (Structuring the Party, 1953) (Taji-Farouki, 1996: 126).[24] After the student has shown a visible change in conduct and way of argumentation and has mastered the basic texts (ibid: 133), she or he may enter the second level of membership by becoming a member. An oath of allegiance has to be taken, in which the new member swears to be loyal to Islam by following the ideology of Hizbut Tahrir and obeying its leadership.[25] According to Osman, the third level of membership is reached when members begin to hold positions in the organisation's hierarchical structure (2009: 10).

---

24 English versions of these and other basic texts (mutabannat) can be downloaded from numerous web pages.
25 For a detailed account of the oath, see Taji-Farouki (1996: 134).

Since 2000, Hizbut Tahrir Indonesia has been organising different public events, ranging from large-scale events such as the 2007 International Caliphate Conference in Jakarta, to much smaller-scale events held on different campuses. Because of this broad range, interested people have the chance to "experience" Hizbut Tahrir events, whether they are obviously declared to be Hizbut Tahrir events or not. I argue that the Internet, for example in the form of *DK.com*, has not only allowed sympathisers and other interested people to familiarise themselves with the organisation's ideas, it has further allowed novices and low-ranking members to actively participate in applying the Hizbut Tahrir ideology and addressing a potentially large public. Innovative applications of the ideology via the Internet target the needs of at least some fellow students by using an appealing and understandable language and making the ideology attractive to young Indonesian Muslims. On the other hand, it also makes it easier for non-sympathisers to critically respond to the various writings of Hizbut Tahrir members in everyday discussions held on campus, as well as in public seminars organized by different Islamic organisations. These processes seem to have the effect of fostering public debate on different campuses and lead to ongoing discussions of what it means to "be a good Muslim".

Conclusion – New Ways for Honing Islamic Virtues

In this article, I have argued that new media technologies, such as the web portal *DK.com*, have facilitated the emergence of new kinds of highly dynamic structures of mobilization, which by default have become less hierarchic. The fluid networks that emerge are more open and inclusive than the organisations whose ideology they reflect. Joining a virtual community demands a minimum level of initial commitment, and everyday activities may not or not yet be permeated by the ideological aims of the organisation at this early stage. As the web portal *DK.com* has been mostly designed by students for students, it is tailored to their needs. It offers schemata that address problems that many perceive to be facing Indonesia and responds to their concerns and frustrations. The advantage to the organisation of having a wide range of authors addressing a potentially large readership is the generation of a wide range of topics related to the ideology of Hizbut Tahrir, ranging from everyday questions about motivation to much broader questions about the reorganisation of resource distribution, the education and health system.

To analyse phenomena such as the web portal *DK.com*, I argue that the mobilisation processes of organisations such as Hizbut Tahrir need to be imagined more dynamically. In particular, we must conceive more fluidly of the category of those who are not formal members – the sympathisers. Rather than dividing this group into sympathisers and non-sympathisers, we might see the people as a set of concentric circles that grow in circumference as the level of involvement decreases. Although "liking" *DK.com* on Facebook is very different from studying actively as a novice in its study circles, the group that encompasses both weak and strong sympathisers is not only important for Hizbut Tahrir as a target group, but also deserves scholarly attention in order to understand trends in contemporary Islam in general. A more dynamic approach in regard to mobilisation strategies and media usage might help us grasp the group's influence beyond the limits of its official organisational membership and also help account for phenomena such as electronically mediated forms of participation that gain considerable support among mainstream organisations, as well.

In their everyday reality as *dakwah* activists, students often face severe opposition to their ideology and have to engage in critical discussions. The public sphere is thus at the same time a space for the normative education of others that the *dakwah* activists pursue, as well as for public deliberation and argumentation. As I have shown, *dakwah* is performed precisely when differences emerge about what it means to be "a good Muslim", and when these discrepancies make argumentation necessary. The form of public sphere I have been discussing thus cuts across the distinction between public and private, as well as between state and society, both of which are central to the Habermasian notion of the public sphere (Habermas, 1962, 1990). Deliberative and disciplinary moments are inextricably interwoven and interdependent within this space. It is thus necessary to analyse media effects on everyday religious practice beyond simply perceiving them as the contradiction between deliberative and disciplinary effects of media.

Bibliography

ALI, A., 2006. Tabligh Jama'at and Hizbul Tahrir: Divergent Paths to Convergent Goals, Education to Counter Extremism. *Dialogue and Alliance,* 20 (2), pp. 51-66.

ASAD, M., 2003. *The Message of the Qur'an.* Dubai: Oriental Press.

BARAN, Z., 2005. Fighting the War of Ideas. *Foreign Affairs,* 84 (6), pp. 68-78.

BRÄUCHLER, B., 2003. Cyberidentities at War: Religion, Identity and the Internet in the Moluccan Conflict. *Indonesia,* 75, pp. 123-151.

BUDIARTI, R. T., 2009. Civitas Akademika UGM Mewujudkan Bangsa yang mandiri, kuat, berpengaruh, terdepan, dan mulia dengan Khilafa (The academic community of the Gadjah Mada University establishes a autonomous, strong, influental, progressive and honourable society under the caliphate). In: C. NEF SALUZ, ed. *Dynamics of Islamic Student Movements.* Yogyakarta: Resist Book.

BUSH, R., 2009. *Nahdlatul Ulama and the Struggle for Power within Islam and Politics in Indonesia.* Singapore: ISEAS.

DAMANIK, A. S., 2002. *Fenomena Partai Keadilan: Transformasi 20 Tahun Gerakan Tarbiyah di Indonesia (The Justice Party Phenomenon: 20-Year Transformation of the Tarbiyah Movement in Indonesia).* Bandung: Teraju.

EICKELMAN, D., 1992. Mass Higher Education and the Religious Imagination in Contemporary Arab Societies. *American Ethnologist,* 19 (4), pp. 643-655.

EICKELMAN, D. & ANDERSON, J., 1997. Print, Islam, and the Prospects for Civic Pluralism: New Religious Writings and Their Audiences. *The Journal of Islamic Studies,* 8 (1), pp. 43-62.

FEALY, G., 2007. Hizbut Tahrir in Indonesia: Seeking a "total" Islamic Identity. In: S. AKBARZADEH & F. MANSOURI, ed. *Islam and Political Violence: Muslim Diaspora and Radicalism in the West.* London: I.B. Tauris.

HABERMAS, J., 1962. *Strukturwandel der Öffentlichkeit Untersuchungen zu einer Kategorie der bürgerlichen Gesellschaft.* Neuwied: Luchterhand.

HABERMAS, J., 1990. *Strukturwandel der Öffentlichkeit: Untersuchungen zu einer Kategorie der bürgerlichen Gesellschaft.* Frankfurt, Main: Suhrkamp.

HIRSCHKIND, C., 2001. Civic Virtue and Religious Reason: An Islamic Counterpublic. *Cultural Anthropology,* 16 (1). Pp. 3-34.

HIRSCHKIND, C., 2006. *The Ethical Soundscape: Cassette Sermons and Islamic Counterpublics.* New York: Columbia University Press.

HOSEN, N., 2008. Online Fatwa in Indonesia: From Fatwa Shopping to Googling a Kiai. In: G. FEALY AND S. WHITE, ed. *Expressing Islam: Religious Life and Politics in Indonesia,.* Singapore: ISEAS Publishing.

LIM, M., 2005. *Islamic Radicalism and Anti-Americanism in Indonesia: The Role of the Internet.* Washington: East-West Center.

MUHTADI, B., 2009. The Quest for Hizbut Tahrir in Indonesia. *Asian Journal of Social Science,* 37, pp. 623-645.

NORTON, A. R., 1995. *Civil society in the Middle East.* Leiden [etc.]: Brill.

OSMAN, M. N. M., 2009. Reviving the Caliphate in the Nusantara: Hizbut Tahrir Indonesia's Mobilization Strategy and Its Impact in Indonesia. *Working Paper S. Rajaratnam School of International Studies Singapore,* No. 171.

ROY, O., 1996. *The Failure of Political Islam.* Cambridge, MA: Harvard University Press.

SCHULZE, F., 2008. Pluralismus und Demokratie im radikal-islamischen Diskurs in Indonesien am Beispiel der Hizbut Tahrir. In: F. SCHULZE & H. WARNK, ed. *Religion und Identität: Muslime und Nicht-Muslime in Südostasien.* Wiesbaden: Harrassowitz Verlag, pp. 23-42.

SIDIQ, M., 2003. *KAMMI dan Pergulatan Reformasi: Kiprah Politik Aktivis Dakwah Kampus dalam Perjuangan Demokrasi di Tengah Gelombang Krisis Nasional Multidimensi (KAMMI in the Struggle of Reformation: The Political Process of Campus Dakwah Activists in the Struggle for Democracy in the Middle of the Multidimensional National Crisis).* Solo: Era Intermedia.

SIVAN, E., 1990. The Islamic Resurgence: Civil Society Strikes Back. *Journal of Contemporary History,* 25 (3), pp. 353-364.

TAJI-FAROUKI, S., 1996. *A Fundamental Quest: Hizb al-Tahrir and the Search for the Islamic Caliphate.* London: Green Seal (Publishing) Limited.

WARD, K., 2009. Non-violent Extremists? Hizbut Tahrir Indonesia. *Australian Journal of International Affairs,* 63 (2), pp. 149-164.

CAROLA RICHTER

Media Strategies of the Major Social Movement in Egypt: The Muslim Brothers' Website *ikhwanonline.net*

The rapid development of information technology during the last decade has fuelled discussions about its impact on political and social changes of authoritarian systems. There has been, for example, a real hype about the use of *Twitter* and *YouTube* by the protest movement in Iran in summer 2009. The German magazine *Der Spiegel* even asked whether the Internet will be able to overthrow dictatorships.[1] Furthermore, the debates about the impact of bloggers in countries such as Egypt, Iran or China as well as reports about the mobilization effects of *Facebook* and other social network media suggest massive media effects on the change of political systems.[2] Not to mention the popular uprisings in Tunisia and Egypt at the beginning of 2011 which have been supported and also covered by mobile phones, blogs and *Facebook*. Although the evidence seems stunning and the regimes obviously fear the mobilizing effects of the internet and mobile technology, claims about media-driven change have to be analyzed carefully. Lynch (2008, 28), for example, emphasizes that media "can not stand in for the hard work of politics: party organization, mobilization, bargaining, and negotiation". Thus, it will be assumed here, that initiating political change in terms of sustainably destabilizing authoritarian systems relies heavily on relevant political actors, their resources and their utilization of political opportunities. Nevertheless, media tend to become one of the major resources of challengers to authoritarian regimes. It seems therefore useful to embed media studies into structural analyses of political systems and its relevant actors in order to identify the real impact media can have on political change. The concept of social movements provides such an integrative interdisciplinary framework.

---

1 „Die digitale Revolution", SPIEGEL 26/2009.
2 See for Iran Michaelsen, for Egyptian blogging Jurkiewicz, and for the usage of Facebook Nef in this volume.

The analytical framework of social movement theory includes three major approaches. First, to identify relevant actors by focusing on the resource mobilization capacities of a movement such as their ability to build social networks or acquire financial support. Second, focusing on structural elements, it can be shown if and how socially embedded movements react to a changing political opportunity structure by reformulating their strategies in order to adapt to new forms of access to political institutions, to changes in the ruling elite or to a shift in the nature of state repression. The third approach concentrates on the movements' framing strategies. Snow and Benford (1988: 198) refer to framing as a tactic used by political and social actors to assign meaning to certain ideas and events in order "to mobilize potential adherents and constituents, to garner bystander support, and to demobilize antagonists".

In this paper, the described concept will be used to examine the media strategies of the Muslim Brothers which represent the main social movement in contemporary Egypt. After describing the development of their media strategies referring to their resource mobilization capacities and their adaptation to changing political opportunity structures, the paper comprises a comparative framing analysis of the Brothers' central media outlet – the website *ikhwanonline.com* – with other Egyptian mainstream media during the debate about the constitutional amendments in spring 2007. This will serve as an example to discuss effects of social movements' media in an authoritarian political system.

Theoretical Remarks: Social Movements, Media Usage and Political Change in Authoritarian Systems

According to Rucht (1994: 338-339), social movements are mobilized networks of groups that try to initiate, prevent or revoke social and political change by means of protest. The main difference of social movements in relation to other political actors such as parties is their general exclusion or marginalization from institutions of political decision-making. This means that the claims of these groups have not directly to be taken into account by political incumbents in order to preserve their legitimacy. Therefore, social movements are obliged to use non-institutionalized means of protest to influence political decision-making (Jenkins, 1995: 15).

Using a concept of Schubert, Tetzlaff and Vennewald (1994) this observation can be transferred into an authoritarian political context, arguing that the struggles for change within a political system are fought out between strategic and contentious groups. Strategic groups represent the ruling elites that compete for a share of power without contesting the rules of the system itself. Contentious groups, on the other hand, are described as potent actors who challenge the status quo when they are able to act autonomously in certain social or political sectors, can withstand cooptation by the regime, appear as a credible alternative to the people or a large part of the people, and openly delegitimize the regime (Schubert et al., 1994: 68-69). Referring to the importance of media, Wolfsfeld (1997: 13) uses this approach to describe the struggle of challengers vs. incumbents as a struggle over media access, arguing that "one cannot, and should not, distinguish between the contest over the news media and the more general contest over political control". In addition, Rucht argues that it is not the direct confrontation between the regime and its challenger that effects the regime's politics but "the resonance that has been provoked by the reflection of the confrontation in the media" (1994: 347).

While obvious change in the political system is the ultimate goal of a social movement, a two-fold communicative strategy seems necessary to reach the resonance that may support this goal – comprising an internal and an external dimension. With regard to the first dimension, establishing and maintaining the internal cohesion of the movement by mobilizing internal resources seem important to gain social power, political relevance and autonomy from the regime. A network of interpersonal communication structures as well as the use of so called "small media" such as cassette tapes or leaflets may suit the transmission of collective symbols and shared values to the followers and support this internal cohesion.

These forms of communication can strengthen internal networking, shape the collective identity of the movement and support the movement's position in order to withstand attempts of cooptation, but it may ultimately lead to what Downey & Fenton (2003: 190) call the "radical ghetto" of the movement's enclave. The authors argue that real effects on political processes can be reached only beyond this "ghetto" because a movement's "value depends ultimately on how influential these enclaves become in the context of the mass media public sphere and formation of public opinion". Thus, the transfer or spillover of the movement's issues, interpretations and strategies into the mass media would increase the pressure on political decision makers to react on these claims (Schmitt-Beck, 1998: 475-476).

With regard to the Arab world, it can be observed that authoritarian systems try hard not to lose control of public discourse. By dominating the media sphere and excluding other actors, the regimes try to secure their position so as to legitimize their political programs and actions and limit public resonance of their challengers. Among the common restrictions placed on political antagonists are: the marginalization of oppositional media by means of obligatory licensing; the cooptation or imprisonment of journalists; or the banning of media outlets (see, for example, KAS, 2008). Thus, one of the important steps for social movements to set up preconditions for political change seems to be a commitment to pluralize public discourses. Access to the public sphere offers the regimes' challengers opportunities to force them to make political processes more transparent and to demand the movements' specific views to be considered in decision-making.

However, it was first and foremost pressure from business lobby groups in most of the Arab and Islamic world that finally led to a guided deregulation of most media sectors. Besides the expansion of the internet, other media such as the press, television and radio were also liberalized since around the year 2000, although this liberalization has tight limits (see, for example, Sakr, 2007; El Amrani, 2006a). However, the internet in particular with its features of de-central organization, interactivity and interconnectivity to other media genres, has opened up new spaces for social and political actors. Internet use, in Egypt for example, has increased massively during the last decade.[3] Thus, websites as well as blogs and social networking sites have been incorporated into different actors' strategies of reaching out to the public in order to overcome their political marginalization and mobilize collective action (compare Jurkiewicz in this volume).

---

3   The ITU states the following progress of Internet users of the total population: 2009 – 24.26%, 2008 – 16.65%, 2007 – 13.95%; 2006 – 13.04%; 2005 – 12.19%; 2004 – 5.37%; 2003 – 4.21%; 2002 – 2.72%; 2001 – 0.87%; 2000 – 0.67%. Source: International Telecommunication Union 2010: http://www.itu.int/ITU-D/ICTEYE/Indicators/Indicators.aspx [Accessed 10 January 2011]

The Egyptian Muslim Brothers and Their Media Strategies

In Egypt, the internal pressure to liberalize the country economically coincided with the United States' pressure to liberalize the Arab political systems during the war in Iraq in 2003. The Egyptian regime, heavily dependent on U.S. financial aid, was obliged to loosen its grip on political freedoms in the country. These changes in the political opportunity structure had also strongly affected the media system, providing political challengers with a wide range of potential communication channels. In 2001, the first privately operated Egyptian TV-channels were introduced. Furthermore, the regime pushed the accessibility of the internet in order to modernize the country without implementing heavy censorship on content and access. Finally, in 2004, the first privately owned daily newspaper, *al-Masry al-Yawm*, received a license followed by dozens of weeklies and monthlies. Thus, the preconditions had been set for challengers such as the Muslim Brothers to make use of these new media.

In this situation, the new leader or "General Guide", Mohammad Mahdi Akif, took over as head of the Muslim Brothers in 2004.[4] Under his guidance, the previous self-centered, inward directed communication strategy of the movement was changed into a pro-active outward directed strategy that openly tries to overcome the marginalization attempts of the Egyptian regime. This meant to keep the traditional clientele while at the same time the masses were approached. As a result, the Brothers made consistent use of the new media to reappear as an autonomous and potent political actor embracing larger parts of the Egyptian public. While several actors and the media close to the ruling regime declare this new approach as an opportunistic strategy to take over political power, it should rather be seen as a paradigmatic shift in the Brotherhood which activated its resources and adapted its frames according to the specific opportunities given in a specific political context.

In fact, the Muslim Brothers had once again reached a decisive point in their development which required a new positioning. During their history, the Brothers often had to adapt their political and media strategies to changing

---

4　Akif remained in office until 2010 when the present guide Muhammad al-Badi' was elected.

political structures. By shedding light on the main characteristics of their performance within these respective structures, the development of their media strategies will be outlined. At the same time, it will become clear how learning processes shaped the current media strategy of the Muslim Brothers.

When the Society of the Muslim Brothers was founded by the teacher Hassan al-Banna in 1928, it was meant to be an apolitical society aiming at social renewal through religious education and mutual aid (Munson, 2001: 488). However, the common anti-colonial tendencies in the Arab world in the 1930s and 1940s led to a broader politicization of the movement. Between 1928 until their prohibition in 1954, the Brothers published no less than 14 consecutive newspapers and magazines, of which *al-Da'wa* was the most renowned (Mitchell, 1993 [1969]: 185ff). On the one hand, these newspapers functioned as fora for intellectual discussions targeting the educated Muslim elite. However, Mitchell argues, that in 1938 Banna initiated the first "political weekly" to support the arising political struggle with the regime. This twofold strategy of discussing the religious foundations of the movement while at the same time trying to activate political participation was constitutive during the founding phase of the movement. At this time, their discourses resonated among large parts of the middle classes as well as among the other political actors such as the Wafd party. Due to its relevance in social services and education the Brothers had established themselves in Egypt with an estimated number of up to a million followers in 2000 regional branches (Krämer, 1999; Zollner, 2009: 10).

Following their tradition of a movement opting for social and political renewal, the Muslim Brothers supported the coup d'état of the Free Officers against the Egyptian king in 1952. However, after al-Bannas dead and under the subsequent General Guide of the Muslim Brothers, Hassan al-Hudaibi, the Brothers became increasingly fragmented because of an unsolved dispute on its further orientation. Thus, when Gamal Abdel Nasser took over power in 1954, he was able to ban the Muslim Brothers, a possible political competitor, and their public outlets completely, restricting their communication to clandestine internal contacts. Thus, public resonance of its goals and ideology was effectively restricted. However, the established social ties prevented the Brothers from falling apart. The Brothers started to re-establish their social work on the grassroots-level refraining from any openly articulated political activity. At the same time, the most renowned prisoner, Sayyid Qutb, gained a strong followership among fellow prisoners with his elaborate anti-governmental ideology. When he was executed in 1966, his writings and prison lectures had fuelled tendencies to fundamental militant opposition among parts of the imprisoned Brothers against the allegedly illegitimate Egyptian regime (Krämer, 1999). As a result, the restrictive political structure during Nasser's regime made the Brothers fragment and oscillate between an ideology of socio-religious education following Hudaibi (Zollner, 2009: 43ff), and revolutionary uprising in the footsteps of Sayyid Qutb, thus lacking a moderate political strategy.

The Muslim Brothers regained limited official toleration only in the 1970s after the new president Anwar al-Sadat strategically positioned Islam as a way to counterbalance the Nasserist political actors. The permission to re-publish *al-Da'wa* as their official mouthpiece of the movement in 1976 marked this accomodationist regime strategy. However, during this period, the Muslim Brothers were not the dominant Islamist actors. While the conservative leaders of the Brothers primarily held on to a focus in social and educational work, newly found Islamic groups at universities gained a strong followership among younger students. They established what Dufner termed a "counter-culture to public institutions" (1998: 28), expressing therewith their opposition to the ruling regime. While the Brothers did not extend their communicative strategy beyond their journals, the Islamic student cells operated a wide range of small media such as wall newspapers and leaflets, they organized conferences, summer camps and cultural events and established independent mosques at universities. Thus, in the 1970s the relative freedom in the political opportunity structure prepared the ground for a new generation of activists. When Sadat massively curbed the Islamic student cells starting in 1979, they became increasingly fragmented. While radical tendencies developed into organizations like the *Islamic Jihad* and the *Gamaat al-Islamiya* that tried to push forward a political agenda by militant means, others established "organic connections" (Dufner, 1998: 54) to the Muslim Brothers searching for a more moderate strategy. This merger of older and newer generations resulted in a slight adaptation of the Brothers' political and communicative strategies to the requirements of political mainstreaming.

In 1981, president Sadat was killed by a *Jihad* member and his successor Husni Mubarak cracked down on the radical organizations. Hence, with the failure of the radicals and their means in mind, parts of the Brothers kept looking for different strategies. Thus, starting in 1984, the still politically-illegal Muslim Brothers established alliances with different legal opposition parties in order to enter parliament via the national elections. In 1984, the Brothers set up an electoral pact with the secular Wafd Party and in 1987, the so called Islamic alliance (*al-Tahaluf al-Islami*) with the Liberals' Party and the then socialist Labor Party was formed. The same piggybacking strategy was used to publish newspapers, for only legal political or social institutions such as parties could apply for newspaper licenses. Typically, the movement used the newspapers of their allies to address the public with an Islamist agenda. Temporarily, the secular-liberal *al-Wafd*, the socialist *al-Sha'b* and the liberal *al-Ahrar* served as mouthpieces of the Muslim Brothers. In the 1990s, the Liberals' party leader conceded one of the party's licenses to the Brothers, enabling them to publish their own newspaper unofficially. The outcomes of this strategy were *al-Nur* and its successor *Afaq Arabiya*.[5] The Brothers published also books and journals such as *al-Manar al-Jadid* (founded in 1998). However, the readership of such publications is limited to an intellectual Islamic elite, while newspapers were meant to target the broad public. However, the Brothers did not pursue this public outreach strategy persistently.

In the 1990s, Mubarak intensified his repressive strategy against Islamist and other opposition groups in order to muzzle any protest against his severe neoliberal economic reforms. While the small Islamist Labor Party outspokenly counteracted the regime's discourses and published with *al-Sha'b* the most powerful opposition newspaper during the 1990s (Wille, 2004), the Muslim Brothers failed to raise support beyond their traditional supporters (Wickham, 2002: 208f.). The established network of public service institutions based on the commitment and financial support of pious Muslims served as the showcase for the movement's aim to reform society (see Clark, 2004). Yet, the necessary public resonance to its ambitions and goals was not reinforced by an adequate media strategy of the movement so as to push the regime to react to its claims.

After these somewhat alternating cycles of reaching out to and (forced) retreat from the public sphere, the idea of becoming a legitimate actor in the political

---

5   The newspaper was banned by the regime in 2006.

arena had consolidated itself among the moderate members of the movement. The liberalization of the economic and media sector at the beginning of the 2000s facilitated the process of developing a media strategy supporting this idea.

Prohibited from owning print or audiovisual media in Egypt, the Brothers focused instead on the multiplying function of the internet. Thus, the Brotherhood's first small-scale presence in the World Wide Web – *Haqa'iq Misriya* (2000) – was developed into a communication platform with different wings. During the first years, the websites were shut down by the authorities several times and the websites' main office was raided. However, the Brotherhood established proxy servers in order to maintain its web space. Since 2002, the website *ikhwanonline.com* serves as the focal point of the internet-network targeting the Egyptian and Arab publics, while the English-language *ikhwanweb.com* targets an international audience.[6] Both websites serve as a mixture of a news portal, a forum for journalistic analyses and a public relations tool. In March 2007, the website *barlman.com* was launched to disseminate news and background information about the parliamentarian work of the Brotherhood's bloc to the public. The network was extended by establishing several websites that aim to attract different audiences such as *egyptwindow.net* functioning as a news portal for the young generation of the Brotherhood (Lynch, 2007) or the website *alswaed.net* (Working Hands) that targets Egypt's "proletariat". In 2007, the movement jumped on the blogging bandwagon after Egypt had become the biggest blogger nation in the Arab world. In addition, most of the regional branches of the Muslim Brotherhood in the 26 Egyptian governorates run their own websites.[7] These serve as a decentralized network covering local events so as to spread information among the interested public and members of the regional branches. Their importance as local information tools became obvious during the presidential and parliamentary elections in 2005 when they posted up-to-date documentation of local electoral fraud. Nevertheless, internal communication to keep the traditional clientele was not neglected: In 2007, the Brotherhood launched the website *ikhwantube.com* that enables young Brotherhood supporters to share videos, while sites such as *ikhwanbook.com*,

---

6   Interviews with Abd al-Galil al-Sharnubi, Head of the Media Committee of the Muslim Brotherhood and Editor-in-Chief of ikhwanonline.com, February 22, 2006 and March 8, 2007.

7   See for example the Alexandria branch on www.amlalommah.net or Kufr Sheikh on http://www.kfrelshikh.com/ [Retrieved on January 10, 2011].

ikhwanwiki.com or *ikhwansearch.com* (set up in 2010) are supposed to provide particular networking fora for the youth.

Besides the development of their own communication outlets, the Brotherhood embraced pan-Arab media. The London based opinion-leading newspapers such as *al-Hayat* and *Asharq al-Awsat*, as well as the Qatari *al-Jazeera* News Channel, all classify news according to their news factors instead of evaluating news with regard to a certain political ideology as the state-owned media do. Therefore, the Muslim Brothers' political struggle against the Egyptian regime is a sought-after topic and has been featured regularly. The guidance bureau of the Brothers reacted to this demand with a public relations strategy. Since the beginning of their electoral campaign in 2005, they provide media training to their high-ranking members and parliamentarians, send regular newsletters to leading journalists and name competent contact persons.[8]

The Muslim Brothers apparently have used the actual political opportunity structure and mobilized their resources to establish the means and strategies to reach out to the broader public and go beyond the "radical ghetto" in order to promote their agenda of political change. However, the actual effects of this strategy have to be analyzed. Snow & Benford (1988: 214) emphasize that "the failure of mobilization efforts when structural conditions seem other-wise ripe may be attributable in part to the absence of resonant mobilizing frames". Hence, on the level of published content, the following analysis will examine the frames presented on *ikhwanonline.com* so as to describe the framing strategies of the Muslim Brothers and discuss its possible impact on public discourse.

Case Study: Framing Strategies on *ikhwanonline.com*

As has been outlined in the theoretical part of this paper, the contest over political power is also reproduced in the contest over media access and content. It has been argued that only capable political actors are likely to establish sustainable counter-discourses that trickle into public discourse and thereby challenge the regime's agenda and mobilize participation. The Muslim Brothers have been regarded a capable actor, representing the main political chal-

---

8   Interview with Mohammad Habib, Deputy General Guide of the Brotherhood at the time of the interview, March 8, 2007.

lenger of the authoritarian regime in Egypt. This challenge is supposed to be reflected in its media and their resonance in public discourse.

Hence, in order to examine the issues and discourses on political and social reform publicized by the Brotherhood and its effects on other media in Egypt, a content analysis of the central website *ikhwanonline.com* was carried out identifying its topics and frames and comparing them with those of the mainstream press in Egypt. As representatives of the mainstream press I selected two state-owned daily newspapers – *al-Ahram* and *Ruz al-Yusif* – as well as two party papers – the secular-liberal *al-Wafd* and the social-liberal *al-Ahrar* – and a daily private newspaper – *al-Masry al-Yaum* – for comparative analysis. These newspapers represent a range of ownership structures as well as differing political currents[9], although they are all "mainstream" in terms of being officially licensed mass media in Egypt.

All articles appearing in these media outlets during one week from February, 13-19 in 2007 were identified and counted using methods of statistical analysis. Then, the most prominent topic covered by all examined media within this week was chosen for an in-depth framing analysis. To do so, the period of analysis was extended to four successive weeks. The central frame was identified for each relevant article featuring this topic.[10] Entman (1993: 52) defines framing on the communicators' side as "to select some aspects of a perceived reality and make them more salient in a communicating text, in such a way as to promote a particular problem definition, causal interpretation, moral evaluation, and/or treatment recommendation". Through intermedia comparison of the identified frames, the framing policy of *ikhwanonline.com* could be examined and its effects on the other media investigated. In this chapter, the debate about the constitutional amendments, being the most prominent topic, will be discussed in more detail.

---

9   At the time of analysis the newspapers sold approximately 250-400,000 copies per day (*al-Ahram*), 1,000-10,000 copies (*Ruz al-Yusif*), 5,000-25,000 copies (*al-Ahrar*) 25-40,000 copies (*al-Wafd*), 50-70,000 copies (*al-Masry al-Yawm*). To get reliable figures of newspaper distribution is very difficult because they are constantly over-estimated by the newspapers themselves. The figures given here are reliable estimates according to statements of Salah Al-Asyuti, manager of *al-Ahram*'s distribution house and Ibrahim Issa, editor-in-chief of the private newspaper *al-Dustur* (personal interviews February 22, 2007 and March 1, 2007).

10 For a detailed discussion of the methodological procedure of framing newspaper topics see Gamson, 1992.

In the first months of 2007, President Mubarak had initiated a process to amend 34 articles of the Egyptian constitution. The ruling National-Democratic Party (NDP), the Muslim Brothers, the secular opposition, as well as civil society organizations, all took part in the discussion on the content of these amendments and the process itself. Despite the broad and vibrant discussion in these organizations which proposed a revision of the suggested amendments, the government held a public referendum in March 2007 resulting in the endorsement of the amendments as initially suggested by Mubarak's NDP.[11] A comparison of the frames used during this discussion in the mainstream media as well as the Muslim Brothers' website reveals their successful use of frame alignment strategies. Using the term "frame alignment", Snow et al. (1986) refer to various strategies of social movements to link their communicated frames to other relevant interpreters' frames of the same event or issue so as to build alliances and widen the basis of its supporters.

The Brothers' framing indicates the use of a threefold strategy in response to the Mubarak initiative and its public discussion (see figure 1 for details): firstly – with respect to the process itself – the movement aimed to counteract the governmental frames which tried to display the amendments as an outcome of a democratic process of public participation. *Ikhwanonline.com* emphasized that the amendments were just a cosmetic fabrication staged by the ruling party (30.0% of all its articles on the topic). Interestingly, instead of displaying fatalism by stating that the amendments were more or less irrelevant for the people (6.0%) – a common trend for non-activist media and an obvious trend in the Egyptian street at that time – *ikhwanonline.com* chose actively to try to delegitimize the regime. Thus, the Muslim Brothers aimed at presenting themselves as a relevant and credible political actor. Hence, at the beginning of the debate about the amendments they even tried to foster public participation in the process. However, the use of the "public participation"-frame decreased tremendously during the debate on *ikhwanonline.com* as well as in the secular opposition paper *al-Wafd* due to the regime's disregard of public demands (14.0% overall outcome, 21.4% in first week, only 5.6% in fourth week).[12] While

---

11 See, for example, "Purple fingers, black bands". In: *al-Ahram Weekly*, 29.03.2007, http://weekly.ahram.org.eg/2007/838/fr1.htm [Accessed 4 December 2009].
12 Development of the use of the frame "Public Participation" from the first week (February 13-19, 2007) to the fourth week (March 6-12, 2007): ikhwanonline.com: 21,4% → 5,6%; al-Wafd: 31,7% → 1,9%.

simultaneously analyzing the frames used in the private press, it becomes obvious that they reflect the share and content of the frames used in the oppositional media. This indicates that the private press attributes a higher credibility to the oppositions' frames than to those of the governments' press. The Muslim Brothers' frame alignment towards a more constructive framing and the near absence of pure fatalistic framing may have added to their credibility.

Frame	Islamist ikhwan-online.com	State-owned al-Ahram	State-owned Ruz al-Yusif	Party-owned/opposition al-Ahrar	Party-owned/opposition al-Wafd	Private al-Masry al-Yawm
1. Process of amending the constitution						
CA are a product of public participation	7	38	28	9	21	8
	14.0%	34.5%	25.9%	23.1%	10.1%	8.3%
CA are only a cosmetic fabrication	15	0	2	7	47	21
	30.0%	0.0%	1.9%	17.9%	22.6%	21.9%
CA are irrelevant for the people	3	0	3	3	3	4
	6.0%	0.0%	2.8%	7.7%	1.4%	4.2%
2. Democracy and civil liberties?						
CA will improve democracy and many sectors of society	0	49	37	2	7	6
	0.0%	44.5%	34.3%	5.1%	3.4%	6.3%
CA endanger civil liberties and democracy	12	1	2	11	72	23
	24.0%	0.9%	1.9%	28.2%	34.6%	24.0%
Suggestions on how CA could really stimulate democracy	8	8	7	6	44	21
	16.0%	7.3%	6.5%	15.4%	21.2%	21.9%
3. Relationship between religion and the state						
National Unity supplants religious aspects in the constitution	0	11	26	1	13	10
	0.0%	10.0%	24.1%	2.6%	6.3%	10.4%
Religion is an inseparable part of the constitution	5	3	3	0	1	3
	10.0%	2.7%	2.8%	0.0%	0.5%	3.1%
Total	50	110	108	39	208	96
	100.0%	100.0%	100.0%	100.0%	100.0%	100.0%

Figure 1: Media Framing of the Debate about the Constitutional Amendments (CA)

Second, concerning democracy and civil liberties, the state-owned newspapers claimed strongly that the proposed amendments would improve democracy and bring about desirable social change in Egypt (*al-Ahram* 44.5%, *Ruz al-Yusif* 34.3%), whereas the Brothers' site and other opposition newspapers criticized the amendments strongly for the possible restrictions they would impose on civil liberties (*ikhwanonline.com* 24.0%, *al-Wafd* 34.6%, *al-Ahrar* 28.2%). The non-governmental media, therefore, started to form a communicative alliance in order to challenge the regime's political propaganda. However, among the opposition forces, it was mainly the Muslim Brothers' media that did not simply oppose the regime but debated *how* the constitution should be amended in order to bring democratic transformation about (16.0%). In contrast to other actors like the oppositional Liberal Party, the media output of the Brothers was accompanied with public discussions, symposia and press conferences so as to attract broad public attention to its suggestions as well as the support of its followers. Besides the Brothers, only the secular *Wafd* Party underpinned its media framing on how to amend the constitution (21.2%) with a specific political program. Eventually, it was this combination of consistent media framing, meaningful suggestions and the existence of an elaborate political agenda that resulted in resonance of the "stimulating democracy"-frame in the mainstream media. Therefore, the articles composing this frame in the private newspaper *al-Masry al-Yawm* as well as in the party newspaper *al-Ahrar* reflected strongly the issues set up in the Muslim Brothers' media and in *al-Wafd*. The private media in particular relied on these oppositional frames because they seemed to be much more passionate and vivid then the government's frames and promised a controversial debate. However, the Muslim Brothers received a somewhat more favorable coverage than the *Wafd* Party. This differing resonance was the result of a major frame transformation of the *Wafd* Party that had opted for a fundamental rejection of the amendment process only in the middle of the debate, after it had offered partial support for the government at the beginning of the process. According to Benford and Snow (2000: 620) such a fundamental frame transformation lacks the consistency that would have been necessary to gain credibility among the public: "the greater and more transparent the apparent contradictions in either realm, the less resonant the proffered framing(s) and the more problematic the mobilization". The Muslim Brothers, however, provided a much more consistent framing of its agenda that resulted in a more favorable resonance in the private mainstream media.

Nonetheless, the Muslim Brothers were also obliged to align its framing in order to form discursive coalitions with other forces in the opposition such as the secular parties. This was meant to deepen the resonance of its strategy to delegitimize the regime. With this in mind, the Brothers overtly refrained from making the issue of the relation between religion and the state a broad subject of discussion (only 10.0%), despite the fact that the proposed amendment for article 5 in the constitution would have major repercussions on the political performance of the movement. In a flagrant attack against the Brothers, the regime changed article 5 so as to prohibit parties based on religious foundations (*marja'iya*). This was accompanied by a campaign led by the state-owned newspaper *Ruz al-Yusif* which framed almost one quarter of its coverage on the amendments arguing against religiously based parties in Egypt (24.1%). At the same time, article 2 of the constitution, which states that Islam is the religion of the state and that the principle source of legislation is the *sharia*, was not amended.[13] However, this obvious contradiction between the prohibition of religious parties and a religious definition of the state was debated by the secular groups and their respective media (e.g. *al-Wafd* 6.3%). The Brothers, on the other hand, realized that this aspect would be a very sensitive issue among the opposition forces and that heavily counteracting this debate would not help the alliance-building process with secular and civil society organizations. Thus, instead of fuelling the discussion, the Muslim Brothers chose to consistently stick to frames of mutual interest with other opposition groups and by doing so tried to broaden its mobilizing resources. Even a heavy-handed series of arrests of leading Brotherhood members and frequent verbal attacks by the government and its media did not weaken their resolve to build discursive coalitions via their media.

While the Brothers' virtual and offline mobilization strategy did not result in substantial changes in the constitutional amendments, its framing and frame alignment strategies used in this debate helped to consolidate the Brothers' role as a reliable and credible political actor in Egypt.

---

13 President Sadat had included this article in the constitution in 1971 (amended in 1980) so as to legitimize his ruling with an Islamic approach. Article 2 reads "Islam is the religion of the state and Arabic its official language. The sharia is the principal source of legislation". For an in-depth discussion about the impact of this article see Muranyi 1984.

Conclusion

While representing a relevant social force in Egypt since the beginning of the 20th century, it was only recently and within its political turn that the Muslim Brothers opted for a strategy of reaching out to the broader public by using the online media. This decision implied an alignment of its internal mobilization strategies towards a more publicly resonant agenda and adaptable frames. Comparative framing analysis of the website *ikhwanonline.com* with the Egyptian mainstream press showed positive effects regarding media resonance.

However, after the end of the period of liberalization starting in 2007, the Brothers appear to be divided in conservatives and programmatic renewers regarding the political mainstreaming strategy and the extensive use of online media to reach out to the masses. In September 2007, for example, the movement internally circulated a party platform draft that was instantly disseminated to the public and was discussed controversially in the different Muslim Brothers' blogs and in the other media (Brown and Hamzawy, 2008). Because this discussion occurred during a time of increased regime repression, some Brotherhood cadres reacted harshly towards the discussants and demanded less public controversy and more internal cohesion. Another example for the ongoing inner strife in the movement was the election of the Brothers' Guidance Council and its new General Guide Muhammad Badi' in 2009/10. It reflected strong internal disagreement about the politicization strategies of the Muslim Brothers. A core argument of the adversaries of this political mainstreaming process was that, despite the Brothers success in mobilization and public resonance, they were not able to fundamentally change decisions and actions of the authoritarian regime. Even worse – the Brothers suffered from mass imprisonments of their cadres and obstruction of their grassroots social work after their success in the parliamentarian elections in 2005. In the parliamentarian elections in 2010 they could not to gain a single mandate due to massive electoral fraud. As a result, the conservative traditionalists secured the majority of the seats in the Guidance Bureau and the new General Guide Muhammad Badi' stands for a generation that opts for pietism and spiritual education instead of establishing a political program and pragmatic political participation (Tammam, 2010).

The public uprisings in January 2011 in Egypt provide an interesting case to follow up on the previous discussion. There are some indications that the

Muslim Brothers and their media strategies in coalition with other social movements have helped pave the way for a more active political culture which may finally be able to really overthrow the authoritarian regime. However, regarding the internal fragmentation in the movement and the high dynamics of such uprisings, it is not yet clear how to evaluate the Brothers' role in this situation.

Bibliography

EL AMRANI, I., 2006a. The Long Wait: Reform in Egypt's State-Owned Broadcasting Service. *Transnational Broadcasting Studies*, 15 (January-June), [online] Available at: http://www.tbsjournal.com/Archives/Fall05/ElAmrani.html [Accessed 2 February 2011].

BENFORD, R. D. & SNOW, D. A., 2000. Framing Processes and Social Movements: An Overiew and Assessment. *Annual Review of Sociology*, 26, pp. 611–639.

BROWN, N. J. & HAMZAWY, A., 2008. The Draft Party Platform of the Egyptian Muslim Brotherhood: Foray Into Political Integration or Retreat Into Old Positions? *Carnegie Papers*, 89, [online] Available at: http://carnegieendowment.org/files/cp89_muslim_brothers_final.pdf [Accessed 2 February 2011].

CLARK, J. A., 2004. *Islam, Charity, and Activism. Middle-Class Networks and Social Welfare in Egypt, Jordan and Yemen*. Bloomington: Indiana University Press.

DOWNEY, J. & FENTON, N., 2003. New Media, Counter Publicity and the Public Sphere. *New Media & Society*, 2, pp. 185-202.

DUFNER, U., 1998. *Islam ist nicht gleich Islam: die türkische Wohlfahrtspartei und die ägyptische Muslimbrüderschaft: ein Vergleich ihrer politischen Vorstellungen vor dem gesellschaftspolitischen Hintergrund*. Opladen: Leske und Budrich.

ENTMAN, R., 1993. Framing: Toward Clarification of a Fractured Paradigm. *Journal of Communication*, 4, pp. 51-58.

GAMSON, W. A., 1992. *Talking Politics*. Cambridge: Cambridge University Press.

JENKINS, J. C., 1995. Social Movements, Political Representation, and the State: An Agenda and Comparative Framework. In: J. C. JENKINS & B. KLANDERMANS, ed. *The Politics of Social Protest. Comparative Perspectives on States and Social Movements*. London: UCL Press, pp. 14-35.

KONRAD-ADENAUER-STIFTUNG (KAS) ed., 2008. *KAS Democracy Report 2008: Media and Democracy*, [online] Available at: http://www.kas.de/upload/Publikationen/2008/dr_egypt.pdf. [Accessed 2 February 2011].

KRÄMER, G., 1999. *Gottes Staat als Republik: Reflexionen zeitgenössischer Muslime zu Islam, Menschenrechten und Demokratie*. Baden-Baden: Nomos.

LYNCH, M., 2007. Young Brothers in Cyberspace. *Middle East Report*, 245 (Winter), [online] Available at: http://www.merip.org/mer/mer245/lynch.html [Accessed 2 February 2011].

LYNCH, M., 2008. Political Opportunity Structures: Effects of Arab Media. In: K. Hafez, ed. *Arab Media: Power and Weakness*. New York: Continuum, pp. 17-32.

MITCHELL, R. P., 1993 [1969]. *The society of the Muslim Brothers. With a foreword by John O. Voll*. New York: Oxford University Press.

MUNSON, Z., 2001. Islamic Mobilization: Social Movement Theory and the Egyptian Muslim Brotherhood. *The Sociological Quarterly*, 4, pp. 487-510.

MURANYI, M., 1984. Ägypten. In: W. ENDE & U. STEINBACH, ed. *Der Islam in der Gegenwart*. München: C. H. Beck, pp. 344-358.

Rucht, D., 1994. Öffentlichkeit als Mobilisierungsfaktor für soziale Bewegungen. In: F. Neidhardt, ed. *Öffentlichkeit, öffentliche Meinung, soziale Bewegungen*. Opladen: Westdeutscher Verlag, pp. 337-358.

Sakr, N., 2007. *Arab Television Today*. London: I.B. Tauris.

Schmitt-Beck, R., 1998. Kommunikation (Neuer) Sozialer Bewegungen. In: O. Jarren & U. Sarcinelli & U. Saxer ed. *Politische Kommunikation in der demokratischen Gesellschaft. Ein Handbuch mit Lexikonteil*. Opladen: Westdeutscher Verlag, pp. 473-481.

Schubert, G. & Tetzlaff, R. & Vennewald, W., ed., 1994. *Demokratisierung und politischer Wandel. Theorie und Anwendung des Konzeptes der strategischen und konfliktfähigen Gruppen (SKOG)*. Münster: LIT.

Snow, D. A. & Benford, R. D., 1988. Ideology, Frame Resonance, and Participant Mobilization. In: B. Klandermans & H. Kriesi & S. Tarrow, ed. *International Social Movement Research. Vol. 1*. Greenwich: JAI Press, pp. 197-217.

Snow, D. A. et. al., 1986. Frame Alignment Processes, Micromobilization, and Movement Participation. *American Sociological Review*, 3, pp. 464-481.

Tammam, H., 2010. The MB's new Leadership: Implications and Limits. *Arab Reform Bulletin* (Carnegie Endowment for International Peace), 17 February, [online] Available at: http://www.carnegieendowment.org/arb/?fa=show&article=30995 [Accessed 2 February 2011].

Wickham, C. R., 2002. *Mobilizing Islam. Religion, Activism, and Political Change in Egypt*. New York: Columbia University Press.

Wille, M., 2004. *Das Ende einer liberalen Hoffnung. Ägyptische Journalisten und Rechtsanwälte zwischen demokratischer Verantwortung und politischer Resignation*. Münster: LIT, Münster.

Wolfsfeld, G., 1997. *Media & Political Conflict. News from the Middle East*. Cambridge: Cambridge University Press.

Zollner, B. H. E., 2009. *The Muslim Brotherhood. Hasan al-Hudaybi and Ideology*. London: Routledge.

Marcus Michaelsen

Linking Up for Change:
The Internet and Social Movements in Iran

When, in June 2009, protests over the results of Iran's presidential elections erupted in Tehran and other major cities of the country, pictures and news of the demonstrations and their subsequent violent repression by the security forces were first and foremost transmitted on the Internet. Digital media played an essential role in informing the international audience about the sudden and massive upheaval of the Iranian people against what they perceived as massive electoral fraud renewing the presidency of incumbent Mahmoud Ahmadinejad. With their correspondents confined to their hotel rooms or expelled from the country as well as local journalists under heavy censorship and arrested in great numbers, Western media had to rely almost entirely on information conveyed by Internet services like Facebook, YouTube or Twitter. As a result, they quickly came up with the narrative of a 'Twitter Revolution' according to which Iran's young and techno-savvy population organised extensive street protests against the regime's religious hardliners mainly by using the microblogging service (Armbinder, 2009; Quirk, 2009; Grossmann, 2009; Pfeifle, 2009).

This approach to the events in Iran echoed a powerful myth that has accompanied the expansion of the Internet since the very beginning. Promising an unhindered flow of information and greater freedom of communication, the medium is constantly presented as an effective tool of democratisation, challenging dominant political forces and their control over the public sphere. Quite symptomatically, the optimistic expectations of the Internet's democratic effects, triggered by its worldwide progress in the 1990ies, have resurfaced with every introduction of new online appliances such as weblogs and the social networks of the so-called Web 2.0 (see also Tsagarousianou, 1998; Alavi, 2005; Schmidt, 2006; Bohnen and Kallmorgen, 2009). Initial, and certainly pioneering studies on media and communication in Middle Eastern societies were also impregnated by this enthusiasm about the potentials of the new medium and reflected the by then prevailing paradigm of considering the Internet as a means to erode existing hierarchies and the information monopoly of established elites (Eickelman and Anderson, 1999).

However, the struggle of the Iranian protest movement in the months after the election to confront a power elite commanding a sophisticated machinery of coercion, stable economic resources, and the mass media has made clear that democratic change is not only about using a modern technology of communication. Various factors intervene in the complex process that is a political transformation. This chapter, therefore, argues for a more nuanced approach to the Internet's possible part in the Iranian endeavour for democratisation, taking into account the socio-cultural and political realities that shape the role and place of the media in the Islamic Republic. The Internet does not always and everywhere acquire equal meaning, as Braune aptly states, for the mere disposability of its technological potential does not automatically generate the same applications and effects in different social settings (Braune, 2008: 63). A necessary contextualisation of Internet use builds on detailed observation that permits to fully understand and reconstruct the ways in which social actors appropriate the medium, forming it according to their specific purposes and needs. In order to develop a realistic and empirically grounded perspective on the utilization of the Internet by political challengers and its possible contributions to their activities, it is furthermore essential to place findings on solid theoretical grounds. Studies on media and political transformation as well as the communication of social movements both contribute to a useful framework for guiding the analysis of Internet use by collective actors in Iran who can be considered part of a long-term movement for democratic change, namely the reformists, the women's movement and the so-called 'Green Movement' that has emerged out of the recent election crisis.

Media, Social Movements and Political Change

Transformation theory stipulates that the formation and propagation of alternative views for the future of society is an essential condition to any alteration of a political system (Merkel, 1996: 315). In this process, social movements play an important role in bringing up new ideas and values challenging the existing order and aiming for broader change. They are essential collective actors within the civil society which is normatively considered as a sphere beyond the realm of the state providing room for the formation of shared interests and a democratic political culture (Cohen and Arato, 1992: 555). Since these movements have usually only limited influence on political institutions, they generally rely on different strategies of discourse and protest in order to gain access to the public sphere as the principal arena for a society's debating on social and political issues. At this, they compete with more powerful actors, like government representatives or political parties, as well as the hurdles that characterise the treatment of information by the mass media (Peters, 1994). Nevertheless, the capability of making their demands publicly and effectively heard is a major factor determining the success of social movements for they need to convince bystanders of the legitimacy of their agenda, gain new adherents and mobilise support (Rucht, 1994; Wolfsfeld, 1997). For this purpose, movements engage in the production and maintenance of meaning, actively interpreting and giving sense to their surroundings and occurring events (Benford and Snow, 2000). Through the 'framing' of social reality, they seek to "promote a particular problem definition, causal interpretation, moral evaluation, and/or treatment recommendation for the item described" (Entman, 1993: 52). This process also plays an important role for the internal exchange of a movement because members have to agree upon positions and strategies. In addition, a strong collective identity based on shared values and a common worldview is essential for these movements as it influences the commitment of followers and their willingness to invest time and other resources (Polletta and Jasper, 2001).

It is obvious that in authoritarian systems like Iran, social and political challengers rarely get the chance to organise and communicate their cause openly since the ruling elites maintain control over the principal means of public communication and suppress undesirable activities of opponents and the civil society alike. If a movement's access to the mass media is blocked, a possible solution is the search for alternatives: a phenomenon that has been amply illustrated by the use of so-called small media such as leaflets, cassettes, and the Eastern European *samizdat,* e.g. amateur underground publications of banned literature that gradually provide a forum for political debate. These media permit the formation of alternative public spheres offering marginalised social actors an opportunity to exchange their views and communicate information regarding their activities. They also strengthen the internal cohesion of political challengers who need to come up with common concepts and positions as well as to organise the production and distribution of the publications. Furthermore, not only the active participation in the communication, but also the consumption of contents circulating within these alternative public spheres create imagined communities with shared values that may pave the way for later political mobilisation. (Rucht, 2004; Sreberny-Mohammadi and Mohammadi, 1994; Voltmer, 2000).

The Internet, thus, seems to present itself as a perfect medium for social movements offering a decentralised and non-hierarchical structure, access to public communication at low cost and free of the usual media 'gatekeepers', as well as a quasi instantaneous and transnational diffusion of information (Hafez, 2005). It has been suggested that the Internet and social movements entertain a mutually influencing relationship in which the different online applications provide opportunities for new and innovative forms of collective action that activists, in turn, have to adopt and implement, thereby shaping the Internet and its utilisation (van de Donk et al., 2004: 6). Nevertheless, research has shown that autocratic rulers not only succeed in limiting Internet use that is potentially challenging but also employ the technology for their own purposes and benefits (Kalathil and Boas, 2003; Alexander, 2004; Zheng and Wu, 2005). Factors like education, media literacy and not least political culture affect the Internet's possible role as a media of dissent too (Hafez, 2005; Norris, 2001).

These theoretical reflections provide a basis for examining the online activities of political challengers in Iran. The main focus here is on the mentioned functions of media communication for social movements: creating alternative public spheres, debating strategies and collective identity within the movement, and mobilising followers and support. A preliminary overview on recent political evolutions and the position of the media in the Islamic Republic will provide a deeper understanding of the Internet's significance for the socio-political transformation in Iran.

Media and Politics in the Islamic Republic

Taking debut in the early 1990s and culminating during the first term of President Khatami (1997-2001), a reform process in the Islamic Republic permitted a cautious strengthening of the republican aspects in Iran's constitution and a relaxation of socio-cultural restrictions. Intellectually, this movement built not only on the more liberal aspirations of the Islamic Revolution in 1979, but also on the ideas of Iran's Constitutional Revolution which, at the beginning of the 20th century, sought to check absolute monarchic power by parliamentary control. However, the efforts of Khatami and his followers have triggered an authoritarian backlash. Supported by arch-conservative clerics in the key bastions of the regime, a hardline faction of the political elite closely affiliated to the paramilitary Revolutionary Guards and the security apparatus has gradually taken hold of all state institutions. The ascendance of Mahmoud Ahmadinejad to presidency in 2005 intensified an already ongoing repression against the main proponents of reform within civil society, especially against women's and human rights activists, intellectuals, students and the press (Arjomand, 2009).

This did not mean the end of the reform movement though. While the key forces of civil society, such as women and human rights activists, students and critical journalists adapted creatively to the new environment and outlived the attacks of the hardliners, the political reformists underwent a strategic reorientation. They realised that the mere focus on democracy and political liberties had alienated them from the lower strata of society who were above all expecting economic progress and social justice – promises of the Islamic Revolution that Ahmadinejad had successfully revived with his populist postures. In spring 2009, the reformists made an impressive comeback when they rallied behind Mir-Hossein Moussavi's candidacy for president. After 20 years of absence from the political scene, the former prime minister managed to present himself as a credible defender of revolutionary values while at the same time addressing hopes for a political opening within the modern middle classes. The decision of the hardliners around Ahmadinejad to abort Moussavi's probable victory through an electoral coup subsequently backed by Supreme Leader Ali Khamenei, and the violent repression against the demonstrating masses of deceived voters have pushed Iran's political evolution into a new phase. On the one hand, the already fragile legitimacy of the regime has been further eroded; a significantly narrowed ruling elite holding to power primarily by means of coercion. On the other, the protests against the rigged election have rapidly evolved into a broad social movement for civil rights demanding transparent elections, freedom of expression and liberation of political prisoners (Bashiriyeh, 2010; Jahanbegloo, 2010).
In the struggle for the reform and democratisation of the Islamic Republic, media and questions of control and access to public communication have always played a major role. The national radio and television organisation

remains firmly in the hands of the power elite and is principally used as a propaganda tool. While private broadcasting media are not tolerated by the regime, the press under Khatami developed into a forum of lively and pluralistic debate. During the first years of the Khatami administration, the number of publications doubled, reaching more than 800, and in Tehran alone, 32 dailies were published in 1998 (Bahrampour, 2005/6; Shahidi, 2007). Consequently, the press became the target of a judiciary campaign supported by conservative factions that lead to the closure of more than 100 publications within five years (Khiabany and Sreberny, 2001). During the same time, the number of Internet users grew rapidly from around 200,000 in the year 2000 to 5.5 million in 2003. Today more than 30 million Iranians are estimated to have access to the Internet.[1]

Without any doubt, there is a direct relation between the clampdown on the press and the rise of Iranian online media as many authors of the closed reform publications turned to the Internet. While the editorial teams of newspapers close to the reformist parties opened up online publications such as *Rouydad*, *Bamdad* and *Emrouz*, dissident journalists forced into exile like Ebrahim Nabavi, Massoud Behnoud and Hossein Bastani continued commenting on political developments in Iran by publishing in different online media. After 2002, the emergence of weblogs opened up an additional possibility of communication which Iran's young population embraced enthusiastically. Since then, blogging has become a remarkable tool of individual, but also political expression. After the closure of the reform daily *Vaqaye-e Ettefaqiyeh*, for instance, several young journalists of this paper opened up the group weblog *Hanouz*, which became a platform for lively debates among the authors, other bloggers, and their readers (Sayedabadi, 2004; Khiabany and Sreberny, 2007).

With the growing expansion of the Internet, the state intervened, restricting an ambitious private sector in order to protect its own political and economic interests.[2] In 2001, all private Internet Service Providers (ISPs) were placed under the umbrella of the Ministry of Telecommunication and had to obtain

---

1 Internet World Stats, [online] Available at: http://www.internetworldstats.com/me/ir.htm
2 In addition to restricting politically and culturally sensitive online content, like the websites of exile opposition groups or pornography, one of the main motivations for reigning in the booming private IT-sector were cheap Internet telephone calls to abroad that the ISPs offered and thereby challenged the monopoly of the state owned national Telecom.

access to the Internet from the state's main provider before passing it to their customers. Furthermore, the authorities developed one of the most substantial censorship systems for Internet content and usage worldwide. Filter software and human resources are combined to monitor and block online communication contradicting the political and cultural guidelines of the regime. Dissenting Internet authors are frequently subjected to juridical harassment and detentions (Iran Human Rights Documentation Centre, 2009). A parallel strategy of regime actors was to actively engage in the use of the Internet and produce their own content. With the religious seminaries in the city of Qom leading the way, government institutions and state-owned firms followed suite, presenting their activities on websites of varying sophistication (Michaelsen, 2006). Responding to the online shift of reformist media, the different conservative and hardline groups have published their own websites and blogs distributing news, political viewpoints, rumours and attacks against opponents. The highly factionalised political landscape of the Islamic Republic, thus, finds its expression also on the Internet. Furthermore, this tendency reflects a historical pattern characteristic for Iran's press throughout the last century: whenever a decline in central state authority provided opportunity, rapidly growing and often ephemeral print publications were used by various political actors to publicly press forward their respective agenda. For a long time, the political commitment of the press retarded the evolution of professional journalism in Iran (Shahidi, 2007).

Debating Reformism Online: The Website *Emrouz*

Facing the closure of most of their newspapers, the Internet has become the major outlet for Iran's political reformers. Online media form the mouthpieces of the different reform organisations while individual authors and journalists use blogs to publish articles that do not find a way into the printed press. In this way, the Internet gave an opportunity to young journalists, who had debuted in their profession during the frenetic period of the reform press after 1997, to exercise and develop their skills even after the majority of these publications were closed and state censorship tightened again. In addition, political events or causes often provide an occasion for the emergence of further news outlets. Before the municipal elections in 2006 and the legislatives in 2008, for instance, several newly founded websites published information on the reform candidates and their campaign. In autumn 2008, an initiative in favour of the renewed candidacy of ex-president Khatami for the next presidential elections took off from a website established only for this purpose. However, the authorities blocked access to most of the reform websites for the Iranian public, thereby severely reducing the number of their readers. Although the censored websites are still accessible to computer-savvy users able to circumvent the filter systems, such practices underscore the fact that the Internet is a "pull-medium": users have to search systematically for the information of their interest. Access to the Internet and the ability to use it as such do not imply applications relevant to political change. The value of these reform-oriented online media, hence, is not to be searched in their impact on wider public opinion but within politically motivated circles with high media literacy and interest in alternative information.

Established around 2000, the website *Emrouz* is among the oldest online media of Iran's political reformers. Close to the progressive reformists, who backed the Khatami government and controlled the majority of the 6th Majles (2000-2004) before being pushed to the political sidelines through a massive disqualification of their candidates by the ultraconservative Guardian Council, *Emrouz* has been frequently filtered since 2003. In addition, a number of journalists and technicians working for the website were arrested and interrogated by a radical branch of the judiciary in 2004, partly undergoing torture and solitary confinement. Despite these restrictions, *Emrouz* continued its publication in order to show presence on the Internet and spread news to reform supporters.[3] An analysis of the website's content of November 2006, a few weeks prior to the municipal elections, gives some insight into the formation of the reformists' discourse and their programmatic reorientation one year after the devastating victory of Ahmadinejad. Compared to other online media of different political affiliation, *Emrouz* publishes a higher quantity of articles, certainly to compensate the blocked access of the reformists to other media. Yet, the website is run only by a small editorial board and does not have the capacity to produce all this content on its own. Most of the articles are not unpublished but selected from other reformist or moderate websites and the few remaining newspapers of similar political orientation. Other texts are editorials or analy-

---

3   Personal interview with Mostafa Tajzadeh, responsible editor of *Emrouz*, November 2008.

ses signed by well-known figures of the reform movement, and published with their name and photo. Consequently, it is the choice and compilation of articles that constitutes a major element of the website's discourse.

The content of the website can be divided into general thematic categories, such as economy, foreign affairs, culture, media and university affairs. A quantitatively important group of articles focuses on the economic and managerial difficulties of the Ahmadinejad administration which, at that time, attracted increasing attention and criticism. The municipal elections though, being an opportunity for the reformists to get a foot in the door of state institutions again, constitute the main topic on the website. *Emrouz* frames this issue from different angles. On the one hand, the website stresses the ongoing formation of a unified reform coalition capable of presenting qualified and experienced candidates, who stand for pragmatic and economy-oriented policies. By highlighting these aspects, the reformists seek to overcome their shortcomings in the presidential elections of 2005: the failure to present a single candidate and the underestimation of economic anxieties in the lower classes of society. On the other hand, the website pays equal attention to the difficulties that conservatives have to face in agreeing on a coherent list of candidates. These problems result mainly from the refusal of Ahmadinejad's self-confident followers to negotiate with other groups within the conservative camp. The articles of *Emrouz* depict the rivalries in detail, thereby contrasting the reformists' rational and consensus oriented approach to the power bickering of their opponents.

While all this appears to be a perfectly normal strategy of election campaigning, one has to bear in mind that this discourse is taking place in an environment with limited democratic qualities. The reformists engage in an unequal competition with the regime's authoritarian factions who dominate the entire electoral process and the principal means of public communication. The website thus highlights topics that are not at all treated by state broadcasting and heavily suppressed in the censored newspapers. *Emrouz* informs for instance about the disqualification of reformist candidates, their limited access to national media, and the possibility of election fraud within the Ministry of Interior controlled by Ahmadinejad's allies. Thereby *Emrouz* not only underlines the disadvantages the reformists are jointly facing and reinforces their sense of unity but also urges the need to act: If a further undermining of the republican institutions in the Islamic Republic is to be prevented, then, an active participation in the elections appears as the only solution. Implicitly, the website refutes other strategies such as civil disobedience or election boycott that are frequently discussed by more radical opponents of the current regime. Taking this position, *Emrouz* confirms the reformists' moderate and democratic identity and their willingness to press for gradual but constant change within the framework of the existing Constitution.

Together with other online media and blogs of similar political orientation that relay, extend and accentuate this debate and the depicted framing of the municipal elections, *Emrouz* thus contributes to the formation of an alternative public sphere. Here, reform-minded participants, as active members of a social movement for political change, exchange opinions, discuss strategies, and negotiate a common identity, thereby laying the ground for collective action.

Women's Rights Activism on the Net[4]

With a history of more than a century, the Iranian women's movement can currently be considered as one of the most dynamic forces in Iran's civil society. The presidency of Khatami provided room for different forms of gender activism and the establishment of numerous women NGOs. However, the failure of the reform government to substantially advance women's rights distanced activists from the political reformists and led to the formation of a more independent movement (Shekarloo, 2005; Mir-Hosseini, 2006). Despite increasing repression under Ahmadinejad, the women's movement has been able to build a broad and horizontal network expanding its outreach to society. It has initiated different campaigns focusing on specific demands that highlight the discrimination against women in the Islamic Republic: The most prominent certainly being the campaign for the collection of one million signatures, calling for a change of legislation that is considered to cement inequalities between men and women; others turn against stoning of women as a legal punishment or demand the right for women to enter football stadiums. A common feature of all these initiatives is their independence from political institutions and donors as well as their reliance on the voluntary commitment of participants. Consequently, the collective struggle against the

---

4   This section is partly based on joint research with Benjamin Stachursky, PhD-Graduate at the University of Potsdam, and will be published elsewhere in more detail.

repressive state, fostering new networks of solidarity, and a pragmatic focus on concrete legal demands has permitted to overcome ideological divisions between secular and Islamist feminists, which had affected women's rights activism in Iran for decades (among others: Fazaeli, 2007; Ahmadi-Khorasani, 2010; Stachursky, 2010).

These recent evolutions in Iranian women's rights activism have been underscored by the growing importance of the Internet for the internal and external communication of the movement. Following the general trend in reform journalism, the women's movement, too, has established a number of online media during the last decade. Various websites like *Womeniniran* or *Zanestan* published articles on women's issues not available in the press. Others represented the different campaigns of the movement, distributing information on the content and evolvement of the respective activities. In addition, many weblogs provided a space for further debate and elaboration. Yet, online content related to women's issues was particularly affected by state control so that activists continuously had to find ways for circumventing the filter mechanisms and frequently changed address and names of their publications. Naturally, the public of these websites was more and more restricted to motivated insiders. In providing new possibilities for internal exchange and expressing solidarity, however, the Internet has gained an undeniable significance for the women's movement (see also Nouraie-Simone, 2005; Khiabany and Sreberny, 2007; Mouri, 2010).

The persecution by the authorities forced women activists to retreat further from public meetings so that online dialogue via emails and weblogs helped to prevent isolation. The Internet allowed for rapidly spreading news about arrests and juridical harassment, thereby facilitating the organisation of defence and, in the long run, avoiding the neglect of detainees' cases. The websites of the movement have constantly published articles about activists held in custody in order to follow up their dossier and maintain pressure on the authorities. This practice proved for instance helpful after the crackdown on members of the signature campaign in spring 2007. The exchange on the Internet has also drawn the different activist groups closer to one another and contacts between women in Tehran and those living in the provinces improved. Although most online media are produced in the capital, they provide a central platform for activists in the rest of the country too, facilitating a debate on content, goals and strategies of the movement. Women from Iran's Kurdish provinces, for example, approached the Tehran-based editors of the

Association of Iranian Women's website (www.irwomen.info) to address the issue of honour killings that was specific to this region only and had hitherto not been discussed on a national level.[5]

In addition, the Internet opened up possibilities for journalists and bloggers to become involved in the movement. Committed women like Asieh Amini, Sussan Tahmasebi and many other activists constantly published information and viewpoints on women's rights on different websites and blogs. The online publication and discussion of news on the signature campaign further attracted young people who had previously been interested in women's rights but whose concerns had never really been channelled into action. Finally, online media helped to foster the creation of a shared identity among women activists. Expressing adherence and solidarity, individual users added banners and logos of the different campaigns to their personal websites, promoting, among others, an initiative against the government's 'programme for social security' that sought to reinforce the Islamic dress code in public. Also, portraits of particular activists on the website of the signature campaign depicted their motifs for joining the campaign and the difficulties they encountered when collecting signatures on the streets, and thereby served as inspiration and support for others.[6]

In selected cases, women's rights activists successfully employed the Internet as a tool for mobilisation. In 2008, they launched a campaign against the 'Family Protection Law', a conservative legislation that was perceived to reinforce current discrimination and encourage polygamy (Amani, 2008). Among other activities, journalist bloggers belonging to the movement published the mobile numbers of parliamentarians inciting readers to call and signal their disaffirmation to the planned law. Other websites provided special protest postcards to print out and send to the Majles. A more important effect of mobilisation, however, can be found on the international level as women's activists are able reach out for international media and human rights organisations through the Internet. English sections on the campaign websites not only inform about the general goals of the movement, but also the cases of detention and repression. In close cooperation with influential supporters in the

---

[5] Personal interview with one of the website's journalists, November 2008.
[6] See the different interviews with young activists in the series "Focus on the campaigner" on the website of the signature campaign (Among others: http://www.we-change.org/english/spip.php?article411).

Iranian exile community, activists inside the country are able to transnationally raise awareness on their struggles and to increase foreign pressure on Iranian authorities. The numerous international prizes Iranian women's activists like Shirin Ebadi, Shadi Sadr and Parvin Ardalan have received in recent years attest to the increasing attention their efforts receive worldwide.[7]

It is certainly true that mainly the repression by the regime, restricting organisational and structural resources of gender activism in Iran, has caused a pragmatic reorientation of the women's movement and its turn to the Internet. Nevertheless, the creative integration of online communication into the activities of the movement allowed for enduring a phase of authoritarian regression as well as developing new and more flexible forms of collective action. In the short period of relative openness prior to the presidential elections of 2009, the women's movement resurfaced with impressive coherence after four long years of repression, approaching the reformist candidates to pledge for a realisation of gender equality during their campaigns. Last but not least, women figured prominently in the protest movement after the elections attesting to their self-confidence and experience in political activism (Kakaee, 2010).

Iran's Election Crisis, the Green Movement, and the Internet

Taking into consideration the utilisation of the Internet by Iranian political challengers examined so far, it is evident that during the presidential election of 2009 and the ensuing crisis, the opposition candidate Moussavi and the so-called Green Movement did not initiate a new strategy of online activism. On the contrary, they could build on habits and forms of politically relevant Internet use that had been established previously. With only limited access to television and the press, controlled by the government of Ahmadinejad, Moussavi's campaign counted on the social capital and creativity of his pre-

---

7   In addition to the prominent example of Shirin Ebadi, human rights lawyer and women's rights activist, who received the Nobel Prize for Peace in 2003, see among others: Olof-Palme-Prize for Parvin Ardalan in 2007, International Women's Media Foundation Award for Courage in Journalism for Jhila Bani Yaghoub in 2009, the U.S. Secretary of State International Women of Courage Award and Amnesty International's Golden Butterfly Award for Shadi Sadr in 2010, and the 'Net Citizen Award' of Google and Reporters without Borders for the weblog of the signature campaign in 2010.

dominantly young followers, thus coining the phrase "every Iranian, a campaign" (*har Irani, yek setad*). In addition to several news websites and blogs that operated along the pattern described above, social networks like Facebook and mobile phone messages became important campaigning tools spreading the candidate's slogans and mobilising for public rallies.[8] After the election coup of the hardliners, these horizontal structures of Moussavi's campaign provided a basis for the emerging protest movement.

With demonstrations forming in Iran and the first repressive countermeasures of the regime setting in, films and snapshots taken by mobile phones and distributed on the Internet became the principal source of information for the international media. News and rumours about the unfolding events were also massively published via the microblogging service Twitter to an international audience. This amplified the impression that Twitter and other social media were the main means of mobilisation within the country. Taking into consideration the heavy restrictions on Internet speed and access as well as the temporary closure of SMS-services that the regime imposed during the days of protest, however, it is impossible to discern the effect that Twitter messages might have had on protest mobilisation in comparison to other forms of social communication, such as telephones and word-of-mouth propagation. Many of the messages on Twitter were reposted again and again, distorting the number of users actually present on the ground. Furthermore, the supporters of the reform candidates were already highly politicised by a polarising campaign which had culminated in spontaneous festivities and gatherings on the streets of Tehran and other major cities during the last 10 days before the actual election. All in all, Twitter seems to have functioned more as a means of transborder broadcasting than domestic mobilisation (see also: Esfandiari, 2010).

This is not to say that selected activists have not made excellent use of these online applications to propagate their cause abroad and inform about the severe human rights violations taking place in Iran. The rapid circulation of information in a network-like, rather anonymous communication structure brought more transparency into the methods of the regime and took pressure from single individuals, making for instance the forced confessions of reform

---

8   Already during the campaign for the presidential elections in 2005, mobile phones had become an important tool of mobilization. As for 2009, the reformist campaigners in Iran were certainly also motivated by the impression that the U.S.-election campaign of Barrack Obama and its apt use of social networks and online media had made worldwide.

politicians and journalists who were paraded as "subversive elements" on Iranian state television a futile exercise. Attracting international awareness and support can certainly be considered a positive outcome for the opposition movement. The online communication on the events in Iran has had a remarkable impact on the Iranian Diasporas who emerged out of decades of disillusionment towards domestic politics and organised worldwide rallies of support. The exchange on the Internet also offers means for the expression of solidarity, thereby contributing to the formation of a collective "green" identity and sustaining the initiative of movement members. Transnational supporters expressed adherence by colouring their profile photos on Facebook in green or by using shared nicknames. When the regime, in December 2009, released a photo of the arrested student leader Majid Tavakoli covered in a *chador*, claiming he had tried to flee hidden under this traditional women's garment, thousands of male supporters responded in a massive act of solidarity by posting pictures of themselves wearing a headscarf. The campaign sparked further debates on mandatory veiling in the Islamic Republic and the role of women within the Green Movement.

With regard to the political evolution in Iran, however, it is important to note that a considerable number of green supporters who are active on the Internet are currently not living in the Islamic Republic and have only restricted influence on the events in the country. The limits of online mobilisation became somehow apparent on 11 February 2010, the anniversary of the Revolution, when expectations concerning the massive appearance of protesters in the midst of official festivities and even the imminent collapse of the regime were running high on the Internet, particularly fuelled by supporters in exile. On the streets in Tehran, however, the opposition found itself scattered in front of a massive security presence. For the activities of the movement inside Iran, again, the Internet is rather significant for facilitating debates and interactions among dedicated adherents as well as a larger periphery constituted by politically aware members of Iran's modern middles classes, searching for information. The opposition leaders use websites and social media to distribute their viewpoints and communicate with their supporters. More and more isolated from their surroundings by the regime's security forces, both Moussavi and Karroubi have published extensive video interviews on the Internet to explain their viewpoints and future strategies. Moussavi's Facebook account has already gained more than 120,000 followers who forward and comment his messages on their part. When Moussavi published the 'Green

Charter', a document of historical dimension outlining identity and goals of the Iranian democratic movement, in summer 2010, he pointed out that the presented ideas had been influenced by an exchange through various networks of communication (Tabatabai, 2010).

Conclusion

After the initial enthusiasm about the Iranian 'Twitter Revolution' had ebbed away in Western media, a second, even more persistent wave of writings was set off in order to clarify, with equal conviction, "why the revolution will not be tweeted" (Gladwell, 2010; Morozov, 2009; Abadi, 2010). By criticising the distorted expectations that using Internet technology would democratise a brutal regime, this explanation also underlined the weakness of the opposition movement whose significance was annihilated by the all-encompassing repression of the state or at least limited to a young, westernised and urban fraction of the population. Placing communication technology in the centre of their argumentation, both approaches somehow missed the point. In the same way as for years the international focus on the nuclear ambitions of the hardliners around President Ahmadinejad had prevented to recognise the evolution of Iran's civil society, ultimately leading to the surprise about the massive protests against election fraud and nourishing unrealistic hopes on a new velvet-style revolution supported by the Internet, the dismissal of social media and the Green movement ignored what was really taking place in Iran: The democratic aspirations that inspired, all along the 20th century, various social and political actors in Iran, have found a new collective expression in the formation of a broad and pluralistic movement for civil and human rights. Emphasising the non-violent, law-abiding and gradual character of their activities, the members of this movement attest to the political maturity that the Iranian civil society and reform-oriented members of the revolutionary elite have gained in the last two decades.

It is thus in combination with the political culture of women's rights activists, journalists or reformist politicians that the Internet can play a role for the democratisation of the Islamic Republic. Only a vital and dedicated social movement will put the communicative potential of the Internet creatively into action and benefit from the technology. However, the significance of the Internet for political challengers is above all a result of the authoritarian control of other media and it cannot replace a lively press or the outreach of radio and television. In addition, the impact of online communication on public opinion is severely limited through the censorship of the state. These restrictions notwithstanding, it has been shown that online communication stimulates the internal exchange of the different collective actors within Iran's movement for democracy. In contrast to the censored mass media, websites and blogs help for the formation of alternative public spheres in which active members of the different movements and supporters debate their viewpoints and agree upon common strategies. The social networks that emerge online open up innovative forms for building collective identities and sustaining commitment. Finally, with regard to the mobilisation of support and followers, the Internet appears to be particularly effective on the transnational level, helping activists in authoritarian regimes to attract the attention of international media and human rights organisations.

Bibliography

ABADI, C., 2010. Iran, Facebook, and the Limits of Online Activism, *Foreign Policy*, [online] Available at: http://www.foreignpolicy.com/articles/2010/02/12/irans_failed_facebook_revolution [Accessed 12 February 2010].

AHMADI-KHORASANI, N., 2010. *Iranian Women's One Million Signatures Campaign for Equality. The Inside Story*. Bethesda: Women's Learning Partnership.

ALAVI, N., 2005. *We are Iran*. Washington D.C.: Soft Skull Press.

ALEXANDER, M., 2004. The Internet and Democratization: The Development of Russian Internet Policy. *Democratizatsiya*, 12 (4), pp. 607-627.

AMANI, E., 2008. From Bad to Worse and Beyond ...Widespread Opposition to Iran's 'Family Protection Bill', *Iran Women Solidarity*, [online] Available at: http://www.iran-women-solidarity.net/spip.php?article430 [Accessed 15 August 2008].

ARJOMAND, S. A., 2009. *After Khomeini: Iran under his Sucessors*. New York: Oxford University Press.

ARMBINDER, M., 2009. The Revolution Will Be Twittered, *The Atlantic*, [online] Available at: http://www.theatlantic.com/politics/archive/2009/06/the-revolution-will-be-twittered/19376/ [Accessed 15 June 2009].

BAHRAMPUR, S., 2005/6 [1384]. *Matbu'at dar dowreh-ye eslahat. Chalesh-ha va tahavvolat* (The Press in the Reform Era: Challenges and Developments). Tehran: Centre for Media Studies and Research.

BASHIRIYEH, H., 2010. Counter-Revolution and Revolt: An Interview with Iranian Political Scientist Hossein Bashiriyeh, *Constellations*, 17 (1), pp. 61-77.

BENFORD, R. & SNOW, D., 2000. Framing Processes and Social Movements: An Overview and Assessment, *Annual Review of Sociology*, 26, pp. 611-639.

BOHNEN, J. & KALLMORGEN, J.-F., 2009. Wie Web 2.0 die Politik verändert, *Internationale Politik*, July/August, pp. 18-25.

BRAUNE, I., 2008. *Aneignungen des Globalen: Internetalltag in der arabischen Welt: Eine Fallstudie in Marokko*. Bielefeld: Transcript.

COHEN, J. & ARATO, A., 1992. *Civil Society and Political Theory*. Massachusetts: The MIT Press.

EICKELMAN, D. F. & ANDERSON, J. W., 1999. *New Media in the Muslim World. The Emerging Public Sphere*. Bloomington: Indiana University Press.

ENTMAN, R. M., 1993. Framing: Toward Clarification of a Fractured Paradigm. *Journal of Communication*, 43 (4), pp. 51-58.

ESFANDIARI, G., 2010. The Twitter Devolution, Foreign Policy, [online] Available at: http://www.foreignpolicy.com/articles/2010/06/07/the_twitter_revolution_that_wasnt. [Accessed 7 June 2010].

FAZAELI, R., 2007. Contemporary Iranian Feminism: Identity, Rights and Interpretations. *Muslim World Journal of Human Rights*, 4 (1, article 8), pp. 1-24.

GLADWELL, M., 2010. Small Change: Why the Revolution Will Not be Tweeted, *The New Yorker*, [online] Available at: http://www.newyorker.com/reporting/ 2010/10/04/101004fa_fact_gladwell [Accessed 4 October 2010].
GROSSMAN, L., 2009. Iran's Protests: Why Twitter is the Medium of the Movement, *Time Magazine*, [online] Available at: http://www.time.com/time/world/ article/0,8599,1905125,00.html [Accessed 17 June 2009].
HAFEZ, K., 2005. Globalization, Regionalization, and Democratization: The Interaction of Three Paradigms in the Field of Mass Communication. In: R. HACKETT & Y. ZHAO, ed. *Democratizing Global Media*. London/Boulder/New York: Rowman and Littlefield, pp. 145-161.
IRAN HUMAN RIGHTS DOCUMENTATION CENTER, 2009. *Ctrl+Alt+Delete: Iran's Response to the Internet*. New Haven: IHRDC. [online] Available at: http://iranhrdc.org/httpdocs/English/reports.htm
JAHANBEGLOO, R., 2010. The Two Sovereignties and the Legitimacy Crisis in Iran. *Constellations*, 17 (1), pp. 22-30.
KAKAEE, P., 2010. The Women's Movement: A Model for the Green Movement, Gozaar. *A Forum on Human Rights and Democracy in Iran*, [online] Available at: http://www.gozaar.org/english/articles-en/Women-s-Movement-A-Model-for-the-Green-Movement.html [Accessed 11 June 2010].
KALATHIL, S. & BOAS, T. C., 2003. *Open Networks, Closed Regimes: The Impact of the Internet on Authoritarian Rule*. Washington D.C.: Carnegie Endowment for International Peace.
KHIABANY, G. & SREBERNY, A. 2001. The Iranian Press and the Continuing Struggle over Civil Society 1998-2000. *Gazette*, 63 (2-3), pp. 203-23.
KHIABANY, G. & SREBERNY, A., 2007. The Politics of/in Blogging in Iran. *Comparative Studies of South Asia, Africa and the Middle East*, 27 (3), pp. 563-579.
MERKEL, W., 1996. Struktur oder Akteur, System oder Handlung: Gibt es einen Königsweg in der Transformationsforschung? In: W. MERKEL, ed. *Systemwechsel 1. Theorien, Ansätze und Konzepte der Transitionsforschung*. Opladen: Leske und Budrich, pp. 303-332.
MICHAELSEN, M., 2006. Howze en ligne: La vitrine virtuelle des clercs de Qom. *Réseaux*, 24 (135-36), pp. 323-345.
MIR HOSSEINI, Z., 2006. Is Time on Iranian Women Protesters' Side?, Middle East Report Online, [online] Available at: www.merip.org/mero/mero061606.html [Accessed 16 June 2006].
MOROZOV, E., 2009. Iran: Downside to the "Twitter Revolution". *Dissent*, 56 (4), pp. 10-14.
MOURI, L., 2010. The Iranian's Women Movement in the 21st Century, *Muftah*, [online] Available at: http://muftah.org/?p=221 [Accessed 2 August 2010].
NORRIS, P., 2001. *Digital Divide: Civic engagement, information poverty, and the Internet worldwide*. New York: Cambridge University Press.
NOURAIE-SIMONE, F., 2005. Wings of Freedom: Iranian Women, Identity and Cyberspace. In: F. NOURAIE-SIMONE, ed. *On Shifting Ground: Muslim Women in the Global Era*. New York: The Feminist Press at CUNY, pp. 61-79.

PETERS, B., 1994. Der Sinn von Öffentlichkeit. *Kölner Zeitschrift für Soziologie und Sozialpsychologie*, Sonderheft 34, pp. 42-76.

PFEIFLE, M., 2009. A Nobel Prize for Twitter?, *Christian Science Monitor*, [online] Available at: http://www.csmonitor.com/Commentary/Opinion/ 2009/0706/p09s02-coop.html [Accessed 6 July 2009]

POLLETTA, F. & JASPER, J. M., 2001. Collective Identity and Social Movements. *Annual Review of Sociology*, 27, pp. 283-305.

QUIRK, P., 2009. Iran's Twitter Revolution, *Foreign Policy In Focus*, [online] Available at: http://fpif.org/fpiftxt/6199 [Accessed 17 June 2009].

RUCHT, D., 1994. Öffentlichkeit als Mobilisierungsfaktor für soziale Bewegungen, *Kölner Zeitschrift für Soziologie und Sozialpsychologie*, Sonderheft 34, 337-358.

RUCHT, D., 2004. The quadruple 'A'. Media strategies of protest movements since the 1960s. In: W. VAN DE DONK & B. D. LOADER & P. G. NIXON & D. RUCHT, ed. *Cyberprotest: New Media, Citizens and Social Movements*. London/New York: Routledge, pp. 29-56.

SAYEDABADI, A. A., 2004. Weblag-haye grouhi, halqe-haye aghazin-e goft-o-gou (Group Weblogs, Beginning circles of Dialogue), *BBC Persian*, [online] Available at: http://www.bbc.co.uk/persian/iran/story/2004/11/041114_mj-asa-iran-weblogs-anniv.shtml [Accessed 14 November 2004].

SCHMIDT, J., 2006. *Weblogs: Eine kommunikationssoziologische Studie*. Konstanz: Uvk.

SHAHIDI, H., 2007. *Journalism in Iran: From mission to profession*. London/New York: Routledge.

SHEKARLOO, M., 2005. Iranian Women Take On the Constitution, *Middle East Report Online*, [online] Available at: http://www.merip.org/mero/mero072105.html [Accessed 21 July 2005].

SREBERNY-MOHAMMADI, A. & MOHAMMADI, A., 1994. *Small Media, Big Revolution: Communication, Culture and the Iranian Revolution*. Minneapolis and London: University Of Minnesota Press.

STACHURSKY, B., 2010. *The Promise and Perils of Transnationalisation: A Critical Assessment of the Role of NGO Activism in the Socialisation of Women's Human Rights in Egypt and Iran*. PhD-Dissertation at the University of Potsdam, 16 March 2010, forthcoming.

TABATABAI, A., 2010. Die „Grüne Charta": Irans Oppositionsbewegung manifestiert sich, *Friedrich-Ebert-Stiftung, Berlin*, [online] Available at: http://library.fes.de/ pdf-files/iez/07348.pdf [Accessed not stated].

TSAGAROUSIANOU, R., 1998. Electronic Democracy and the Public Sphere: Opportunities and Challenges. In: R. TSAGAROUSIANOU & D. TAMBINI & C. BRYAN, ed. *Cyberdemocracy. Technology, Cities and Civic Networks*. London/New York: Routledge, pp. 167-178.

VAN DE DONK, W. & LOADER, B. D. & NIXON, P. G. & RUCHT, D., ed., 2004. *Cyberprotest: New Media, Citizens and Social Movements*. London/New York: Routledge.

VOLTMER, K., 2000. Massenmedien und demokratische Transformation in Osteuropa. In: H. D. KLINGEMANN & F. NEIDHARDT, ed. *Zur Zukunft der Demokratie. Herausforderungen im Zeitalter der Globalisierung.* Berlin: Edition Sigma, pp. 123-151.

WOLFSFELD, G., 1997. *Media and Political Conflict. News from the Middle East.* New York: Cambridge University Press.

ZHENG, Y. & WU, G., 2005. Information Technology, Public Space, and Collective Action in China. *Comparative Political Studies*, 38 (5), pp. 507-36.

FREDERIK HOLST[1]

Challenging the Notion of Neutrality – Postcolonial Perspectives on Information- and Communication Technologies

A childhood friend of mine asked me years ago why he always had trouble finding scissors, corkscrews or can openers that he could use and whether this was just to show him each and every day that he was 'different'. He was left-handed and back then in the 1970s, although children were no longer 're-educated' to become right-handed, kindergartens and schools were often still not adequately equipped with tools for the left-handed. I could see his problem, but I thought that it is impossible to make it right[2] for everyone and in this case the majority is right-handed. Still, we asked ourselves who was to blame, if anyone or anything: The inventor of the corkscrew? The people who made right-handed scissors popular? Or the shops that didn't sell can openers for the left-handed? However, we couldn't really find a good reason for any involved party to discriminate against left-handed people intentionally. After all, these tools, the screwdriver, the corkscrew or the can opener were just that: tools. Tools are there to make your life easier, and as long as you do not abuse them, they are not meant to bring harm. At least that is what I thought back then.

Fast forward to the present: Today, we may not even realize the existence of all the technological tools and frameworks that influence our daily practices. Despite having been an IT consultant and internet programmer in my pre-academic life, I am no longer able to keep up with most developments in this field (and maybe a mechanic who has to repair one of these modern cars that you 'fix' by connecting a laptop to the engine can sympathize with me): I do not know the design of the IPv6 TCP/IP protocol that takes care of the e-mails

---

1   I am grateful for comments by Christoph Haug, Sumit Mandal, Antje Mißbach, Saskia Schäfer and Nadja-Christina Schneider. Although not all of them may agree with my analysis in this article completely, their feedback has helped me significantly to approach this topic.
2   Pun not intended back then.

I exchanged in preparation for this chapter. I wouldn't even know nowadays through which processes and protocols the keys that I press on the keyboard are transformed into electronic information, transported through processors and finally end up as characters on the screen only a fraction of a millisecond later. But even though I do not understand these complex technologies, they still 'do their job' for me, no matter if I am a white-western-heterosexual male or a black-subaltern-queer person. Technologies and tools are 'neutral' in a sense that they neither influence nor make decisions nor take sides nor discriminate. Or do they?

In this chapter, I want to take a closer look at the impact of Information and Communication Technologies (ICT) and argue that these technologies are as much carriers of meaning and ideologies as the content they relay, especially in regard of an often underestimated impact on postcolonial societies. Just as my left-handed friend experienced on a much smaller scale, ICT can symbolize and reinforce positions of power, status and situatedness. To address these issues in marginalized societies and communities, a postcolonial perspective shall be taken into account in order to emphasize the specific characteristics of the impact of ICT in these environments. While there do exist models like the path dependence theory that is applied in a number of disciplines such as social sciences, history or economy (see for example Arthur, 1994; Mahoney, 2000) which explain the prevalence of some (technological) developments over others, there is still only limited consideration for the specific impact on postcolonial societies. Postcolonial approaches cover a wide range of contexts and applications, but a common theme often overlooked in other disciplinary approaches is questioning power structures, especially in relation to the center and the periphery, as well as which forms of emancipation can emerge from this (Franzki and Aikins, 2010: 14). An approach limited for example to the combination of media and communication studies as well as area studies may risk underestimating or even ignoring the said power structures. However, it is imperative to keep in mind that the 'online' world eventually reflects 'offline' structures of power, wealth and knowledge. Thus, a postcolonial perspective embedded in a trans-disciplinary framework will help to locate "contemporary phenomena in need of new modes of analysis and requiring new critiques" (Anderson, 2002: 643). This combination shall therefore be applied in this chapter to highlight intersections of and impacts on knowledge flows, technological developments and cultural perception of the self and others in regions and areas that have experienced marginalization. In practical terms, the question of adjusting technology – and not just content – to local demands and settings is of importance and shall be looked at in this chapter with a focus on the impact on language and script. While postcolonial literature has advanced the breaking of binary dichotomies and has shown that both the colonized and the colonizers are affected in the process, the focus of this chapter shall lie on the impact of ICT on marginalized societies in the Global South. For one, this has been a neglected field of research, especially in regard to the technology transfers and the underlying technological blueprints. In addition to that, while there are notable influences in the development of ICT that originate among others from former colonies, such as India for example, the balance of power in this respect is far from equal as shall be shown in this chapter.

ICT, the Disciplines and Postcolonial Perspectives

Coming back to the question of neutrality, the initial assumption that technologies of whatever kind have a neutral influence on their environment may be a no-brainer at first for scholars who generally treat hardly anything as neutral. Philosophers who have made an impact across the disciplines, such as Foucault or Heidegger, have highlighted this aspect long before ICT became prevalent to this extent: One of Foucault's (1977) arguments discusses the decisive impact on social relations that architecture and concrete buildings can have, despite being inanimate structures; and Heidegger states quite clearly that we approach technology "in the worst possible way when we regard it as something neutral" (Heidegger, 1977: 4).

However, when it comes to the analysis of ICT, a problem arises: It is actually two aspects in one. Semantically, it only refers to the technology that is used to transmit information and communication. Yet as ICT has enabled new flows of communication in the last twenty years, it is no longer just the impact of the technology, i.e. the means and modes of transmission, that is analyzed, but it is also the impact of the content, i.e. the actual information and communication being transmitted, that becomes a focus of attention. Therefore, it generally does not lead to raising eyebrows if research on the impact *of* ICT (or, equally ambiguous, "the internet") solely deals with the impact of the *contents* transmitted *via* ICT.

Whether technology or content is at the center of attention often seems to depend on the disciplinary background of each individual scholar, and it can be assumed that disciplines leaning towards the sciences, for example some segments of media and communication studies, are more likely to focus on the technology whereas in the humanities such as cultural studies, area studies or postcolonial studies where culture, literature and language are points of reference, the impact of the content seems to play a more important role. The underlying risk is that the aspect of ICT which is not part of the analysis remains underestimated, thus becomes 'neutral' through negligence. This underlines the necessity of an interdisciplinary approach to encounter ICT beyond mere lip service.

While there have been significant intersections between media and communication studies on one side and gender studies, psychology or history on the other, the same can not be said for postcolonial studies, as Fernández argues. She states that it is "striking that postcolonial studies and electronic media have developed in parallel to one another but with few points of intersection" (Fernández, 1999: 11).

However, this lack of intersection does not stem from a divisive rift that would prevent a common perspective. On the contrary, interconnecting these approaches is important to bridge the apparent disciplinary gap. This is a necessary precursor to fully grasp the complex realities that the entanglement of ICT and diverse societies produce. The so-called digital divide is a case in point: Addressing merely the lack of access to ICT by means of the underlying technology falls as short of grasping the subject as an isolated focus on the lack of knowledge and information would.

More than ten years have passed since Fernández' critical analysis of the state of research, but it seems that a number of points she has raised are still relevant and require further investigation. This is not to say that there have not been significant interdisciplinary approaches in this field. Given the fact that it took quite some time for electronic dimensions to become recognized as fields of 'serious' academic research, Fernández (1999: 13-15) mentions aspects where media theory has already influenced other disciplines, for example gender studies, psychology and history – and vice versa. The late 1990s and the globalization of IT industries has even led to an interest in applying cultural studies in the field of software engineering (Gunzenhäuser et al., 2001). However, a dedicated postcolonial perspective on ICT is still rather uncommon. Those scholarly contributions that do apply postcolonial question frameworks to media theory, such as Poster (2007), somehow do not focus on analyzing the impact of the "T" of ICT. This is remarkable as the hype around the exponential growth and the previously unimaginable possibilities in terms of exchange of information and communication in the mid- and late 1990s have provided for a rather uncritical academic and popular discourse in which the underlying technologies were seen as "either value-free or inherently liberatory" (Fernández, 1999: 11).[3]

Yet ICT can hardly be value-free as their impact on everybody's life does not occur in a detached environment but takes place against the backdrop of distributions of resources in the real world. Coming back to the above example, limiting the digital divide to access to technological infrastructure and information would be masking the impact that the transfer of technology and the therefore required knowledge effectuates. These flows of technology and knowledge have mirrored similar patterns that have been a central pillar to sustain notions of colonial superiority in the past – and often they still do. Back then, advanced technologies were not only sustaining military dominance, but new modes of transport and communication can also reinforce perceptions of the colonized people's backwardness and vulnerability. As these technologies also have become yardsticks for development, the function of technology constitutes an important question when applying postcolonial perspectives of structural inequalities.

With these preliminary thoughts in mind, the utopianism that is expounded in writings such as Friedman's "The World is Flat" (2005), in which it is assumed that the world has or will become "flat" (i.e. 'fair') through ICT, is therefore not merely projecting an idea of a desirable since equitable future which may be

---

3   It would be hypocritical to exempt myself from this perception at that time. Having experienced the emergence of ICT in the mid- and late 1990s as an internet programmer and a student of primarily communication studies, the idea that presumably free access to information and the resulting exchange of ideas would increase human empathy and understanding, was beguiling. Contrasting this perception was a formative seminar in critical psychology on identity and virtual realities at the Psychological Institute (PI) of the Freie Universität Berlin in 1996/97, conducted by Ernst Schraube and Heinrich Schwarz, which was an early eye-opener to understand the multi-faceted implications of ICT in a more meaningful way.

facing various yet surmountable obstacles in the process of realization. This perception is rather glossing over if not reinforcing or intensifying "imperialist initiatives in the guise of utopianism" (Fernández, 1999: 12). While there are nowadays a number of important centers of IT development in the Global South, for example in India, China, Taiwan or Singapore, which have achieved a standing of their own, the question remains in which ways technology and its associated objectives, including design and knowledge of application, evoke and reflect on experiences that reinforce associations of inferiority, especially in marginalized or postcolonial societies. The following examples centered on the localization (i.e. the adaptation of technology to local environments) shall illustrate that the mere fact of having localized access to ICT does not necessarily mean equal standing or prerequisites.

A Short History of Localization of ICT

Today, we take it for granted that a person who speaks and writes Arabic can use an operating system in his or her mother tongue due to the internationalized Unicode character set; that there are keyboards available that reflect non-Latin alphabets and that writing from right to left or top to bottom is no insurmountable barrier anymore either. With the exponential development in the IT world, the times in which users were forced to use, read and write in the languages of the large global markets – and most of the time this was and still is English – may seem long gone. However, most of the said features were only widely available from the mid-1990s onwards, and often only through the use of complex workarounds or additional software.[4] Prior to that, computer and internet access have been pretty much an English language affair where even other Latin-based scripts were implemented rather provisionally than professionally.[5] Even today, many non-European languages are only implemented up

---

4 For example, the Microsoft Windows operating systems only supported right-to-left languages at system level from Windows 2000 onwards. The Microsoft Office suite incorporated a rudimentary support in its 97 edition. When it comes to official language support, Office 2000 still catered mainly to the European/English speaking market: From the over 30 available language versions and proofing tools, only Chinese, Hebrew, Japanese, Korean were non-European languages. Standardized Unicode integration which provided for a relatively easy access to non-Latin script also only took place in Windows 2000.

5 The long-time standard 7-Bit ASCII (American Standard Code for Information Interchange) contains no diacritic characters, such as "ä", "ö" or "ü". In the 1980s and

to a certain level while other parts are based on one of the few full-language versions that are often synonymous with the language of the former colonial powers.[6]

If we take this Arabic-speaking person ten years further back, to the end of the 1980s or even the beginning of the 1990s, he or she would, in order to use a computer, not only have to adapt to the Latin alphabet and script, but as a matter of course also speak English to make use of the technology. For one, because soft- and hardware manuals that went beyond the level of setting up a computer were written mainly in English (or maybe German, French or Spanish), but also because at that time, using a computer in Arabic for anything else but rudimentary word-processing was virtually impossible. So while for a consumer using a computer without substantial knowledge of English was a possibility, anything else in the direction of creating software or adjusting it to local needs, was not.

Thus, if we take three individuals at that time, merely 20 to 25 years ago, who speak three different languages such as English, French and Arabic, the initial conditions in approaching ICT for the three would have been quite different. Even with a similar socio-economic background, the hurdles to access and make use of ICT (despite the varying degrees of operability for each language context) are significantly higher for the Arabic-speaking person compared to

---

1990s, so-called codepages were used in text-based operating systems such as MS-DOS. Codepages were basically translation tables for each (mainly Latin-based) language so that non-ASCII characters could be displayed on the screen. Reading and writing text in different languages became thus possible but the character switch affected the system as a whole, which had the effect that reading a text in Cyrillic led to other characters on the system being displayed in Cyrillic as well (not translating the terms into Russian though!).

6   For Microsoft Windows, an English or French base language edition is still required for most non-European languages. See here for a full list: http://windows.microsoft.com/en-US/windows/downloads/languages-xp. While some European languages such as German are implemented to cover 100 percent of the operating system's dialogues, languages like Arabic are implemented only up to 80 percent where the remaining 20 percent are taken from the French base language edition. For smaller language groups, it becomes even more mixed up: The Bosnian language edition is implemented up to 20 percent on the basis of Serbian language edition which itself is still based to 20 percent on the English base language edition. See http://technet.microsoft.com/en-us/library/dd744336%28WS.10%29.aspx. Open Source operating systems like the various Linux derivates do provide a substantial amount of localization, but as these systems comprise of a multitude of programs coded by different authors or groups of authors, localization can only go as far as the community is willing and able to.

the English- or even the French-speaker, as not only a new language, but also a new script needs to be learned (Mohd et al., 2005). This is not to be underestimated as the additional barriers also make it harder to build expertise in ICT beyond just using a computer. In Europe and the U.S in the mid-1990s, the large number of IT-savvy youngsters who filled the positions in the IT departments of the emerging 'New Economy' were often self-taught programmers (like the author) who appropriated programming skills in their teenage years by exploring the possibilities of the computer in an experimental way. This was possible because language and cognitive barriers were relatively low, as programming languages are generally based on English and written in Latin characters.[7] I wonder if I or any of my former colleagues would have done the same if prior to writing even the simplest 'hello, world' program, we would have had to learn first how to read and write, for example, Arabic or Thai.

The 'Neutrality' of Technology and the Cost of Localization

Of course, the underlying technology at the level of hardware does 'understand' neither English, nor French nor Arabic. All it can deal with are binary states of memory cells that can be either one or zero. In the stone age of information technology, these were represented through punch cards which obviously made programming a very abstract and error-prone task. With growing complexity and processing power, programming languages were implemented that made writing programs more and more like writing sentences, albeit in very rudimentary forms. So while on the level of hardware there are still the ones and zeros that transport our e-mails, the high-level abstraction layers in the form of programming languages are almost naturally in English.[8] Alphanumeric characters, irrespective of their origin, are thus also merely represen-

---

[7] There have been localized versions of a few programming languages, such as LOGO, but these could often not be used for more demanding tasks.

[8] The fact that most programming languages are based on English shows a dilemma: On the surface, sincere efforts are being undertaken to provide more or less acceptable localizations of software for end-users all over the world. However, under the hood, the closer one gets to the core of the system, localization is simply not possible. Not only are there already too many 'dialects' within a given programming language. Localizing a programming language and to substitute the English command *print* with the German term *drucken*, the Malay *tulis* or the Thai พิมพ์ would, just as in real life, create a new language. Source code would only be exchangeable and collaboratively worked on within the users of each language which, even if it was done, would be highly unfeasible.

tations of bits and bytes that need to be stored and accessed in an efficient way.[9] The smaller the character set is, the less storage space and memory it requires. For that reason, seven and eight bit character encodings, such as ASCII and ISO 8859 were for a long time the most widely used ones. Other encodings, especially those that had to represent more than 128 or 256 characters respectively (such as Unicode) require more capacity and were thus economically not viable for quite some time. Three examples for non-Latin based scripts shall demonstrate the practical consequences of this legacy:

For one, this helps to explain why English and Latin characters are still often used on mobile phones when sending text messages via Short Message Service (SMS) in non-Latin-based scripts, for example in Thai or Arabic, despite the fact that suitable keyboards have been available for quite a while. When the SMS standard was formulated in 1991 by the European Telecommunications Standards Institute (ETSI), there were no phones that could display non-Latin characters in the first place, so the need to include these characters (or make more room for them) did not arise.[10] When mobile phone communications in these markets emerged and especially SMS became an important aspect, a solution was required that would have to be based upon the existing standard, as compatibility needed to be maintained. The result was to take a Unicode-based character set that included non-Latin-based scripts, but at the cost of a reduced message size, as the encoding of scripts containing more characters inevitably uses more space.[11] Thus, whereas SMS messages written in the ASCII-based Latin alphabet can contain up to 160 characters, this size is restricted to 70 characters otherwise. This means that a text message with 150 non-ASCII characters will be split in three messages (70 + 70 + 10) and therefore cost three times as much as one written with plain ASCII-Latin characters. Hence, users sending messages in non-Latin script are bound to switch to

---

9 One byte is the basic addressable element in computer architecture. It usually consists of eight bits whereas one bit represents one binary digit, zero or one. Eight bit can therefore contain $2^8 = 256$ different values, seven bits $2^7 = 128$ values respectively.
10 See ETSI documents GTS 03.40 and 03.41.
11 The UCS2 encoding used for non-Latin scripts is based on a 16-bit character size, thus using more than two times of transmission capacity, whereas otherwise an ASCII-based 7-bit encoding is used. As each SMS can contain up to 1120 bits (140 bytes), the resulting length of each message is therefore 1120 / 7 = 160 characters for Latin-based scripts in contrast to 1120 / 16 = 70 characters for non-Latin scripts.

English or a respective Romanized version of the script in order to save money on longer text messages.

The introduction of Internationalized Domain Names (IDN) showed a similar problem: In order to provide users the possibility to enter an internet address (Uniform Resource Locator, URL) in the browser directly using their familiar script, several network information centers (NIC) have begun allowing non-ASCII characters when registering domain names. However, changing all internet servers in the world to understand a variety of non-Latin-based scripts was not an option, again due to financial and compatibility reasons. What was done instead was to change the client software (the internet browser for example) to convert an IDN into a Latin-based name which will be the name that the internet servers will be working with.[12] Unfortunately, this encoded domain name not only has hardly any resemblance with the original representation and is thus hard to remember for users who have to use non-IDN-capable software.[13] It also reduces the amount of characters that can be used for a domain name as a result of this encoding process. The maximum number of 63 (Latin) characters – which are usually far sufficient – decreases the more non-Latin characters are used for the domain name, similar to the SMS issue described above. Yet this approach also contains a drawback that may run counter to its original conception: While IDN may be beneficial for users of the respective local script, it creates new boundaries for users who want to access these localized contents, but do not possess a keyboard with the required characters to enter the URL in the first place. This may not only affect foreigners but also the local population which may not have access to a localized keyboard as these are often more expensive. Thus localization of hardware may create a double bind in some aspects regarding the idea of greater integration of ICT use and the exchange of information.

Last but not least, the earlier mentioned relatively late inclusion of non-Latin-based scripts in operating systems can also be attributed to a combination of

---

12 See RFC3490 "Internationalizing Domain Names in Applications (IDNA)", http://datatracker.ietf.org/doc/rfc3490/.
13 The URL of the Egyptian Ministry of Information can be entered in its Arabic form as http://مصر.الاتصــــالات-وزارة.موقــع/, but then gets internally translated to http://xn--4gbrim.xn----ymcbaaajlc6dj7bxne2c.xn--wgbh1c/. A single diacritic character in the URL http://www.dömain.de translates the whole URL to a significantly different http://www.xn--dmain-jua.de.

outdated standards kept for compatibility reasons and simple lack of memory and storage space. In present times where RAM and hard disk capacities are beyond human comprehension, it no longer matters whether a text file is several kilobytes or megabytes large. But about fifteen years ago, when storage capacities were about one thousandth of current capacities, it surely did matter. The lesser amounts of bits and bytes that were used, the better and more efficient a system was. Likewise, the lesser characters that needed to be encoded the more text could be stored in the same amount of storage capacity. Making Unicode a standard became only feasible once users would no longer complain any more that their files would take up double the amount of space on the hard disk.[14]

Implications for Postcolonial Societies

These examples show that there are concrete impacts on the people who have to use these technologies – and that the design of a technology and the conventions on how to use it – the technological blueprint – has different consequences for people with a different linguistic background. I argue that these technological blueprints, often originating from countries that were former colonial powers, and their respective implementations not only carry economic, but also socio-cultural inclinations. These have significant impacts on perceptions and developments on postcolonial societies, and the technological restrictions explained before are not the only implications in this respect. Turning a blind eye on these implications leads to a false notion of neutrality of technology – or as Suchman (2002: 140) refers to it "the fallacy of the empty vessel": "mistaking one's own ignorance of what exists elsewhere – knowledge, information systems, practices – for their absence". More important than the question whether it may have been ill-intent, negligence or simply unawareness is the fact that the adaptation of these blueprints in the former colonies has and probably could have never been questioned. Back then as well as nowadays the socio-economic pressure to embrace these technologies is still overwhelming, albeit not always beneficial: A Laotian using Latin-based

---

14 Unicode encodings exist in variations using – generally speaking – 16 to 32 bits (two to four bytes) per character which results in document sizes at least doubling, if not quadrupling compared to ISO 8859 encodings.

characters instead of Lao when writing an SMS text message may realize that this is economically more viable, but at the cost increasing ambiguities due to the lack of tonality, a central feature in Lao and other Asian languages. The same goes for the English-language keyboard layout for typewriters and computers which is still used in many former colonies despite layout inconveniences in relation to local languages. Although in Malaysia for example, there have been proposals for localized keyboard layouts which are more ergonomic to use, the idea nevertheless did not gain a strong foothold so far and is unlikely to become economically viable in the future (Khan et al., 2006).[15]

These developments can lead to a deprecation of one's own language or script as I could witness during a field trip in Vietnam in 2002: I had encountered a student on a bus ride who told me he was grateful to the French that they introduced a Romanized script and did away with the Chinese-based characters. Asked why he was happy about it and whether it was because of the complexity of Chinese characters, he replied that it was not so much the complexity of the characters (which he had learned anyway), but because this helped the Vietnamese to learn languages such as French and English more easily and thus become more competitive in the global market compared to other nations in the region. These priorities that put competitiveness over cultural and linguistic aspects underline not only the threatened position of marginalized languages, but also show how the perspective on colonial rule and self perception may be affected.

The implementation of languages in ICT contexts leads to another aspect where hierarchies come into play, namely how decision-making processes are structured when dealing with the languages of postcolonial societies. Taking the above-mentioned example of the development of Unicode which was

---

15 The prevalence of keyboard layouts is actually one of the most prominent examples of path dependency theory in the field of economics. According to David (1985), initially, technical hardware requirements were partly responsible for the QWERTY layout. When these requirements no longer needed to be met, for example in computer keyboards, the QWERTY layout was kept nevertheless despite more ergonomic systems such as Dvorak. According to David, the quasi-irreversibility of this development is based among other reasons upon the very high costs of switching to a different system, both in terms of financial and human resources. While it is no doubt difficult and costly to change an established system, the issue remains that a localized system could never be established in the first place, as was the case in several European countries, such as France or Turkey.

widely seen as a means to enable a large number of people to use local scripts, the decisions by the Unicode consortium regarding what characters make it into the set and in which order are at times questionable. The largest bone of contention is the so-called "Han unification" where Chinese, Japanese and Korean characters which have a common linguistic basis and history were unified in the process of including them in the Unicode character set. To put it simple, the 'problem' with these scripts is that two characters may have the same meaning but are written in a different way, and some of the lesser used variants did not make it to the Unicode set. While this does not affect most aspects of everyday use, older texts may suffer from this, and, as Zhao and Baldauf state, "to ancient canon researchers and digital library/museum developers, this kind of unification is parallel to some letters on the keyboard missing for alphabetic language speakers" (Zhao and Baldauf, 2008: 316). The reasons for this may be due to technical requirements and the application of an underlying encoding logic that will have to make compromises when merging letter- and character-based scripts in one set. However, the fact that especially historical characters become more difficult if not impossible to be reproduced is seen by some in the region as an attempt to streamline the languages and has resulted in resisting Unicode in China and Japan where alternative character sets have emerged that now stand in competition with Unicode. In addition to that, rivalries between China and Japan are also fought out against this backdrop (Zhao and Baldauf, 2008: 319). Last not least, it needs to be acknowledged that the fact that an outside entity (the Unicode consortium is based in the United States) is 'organizing' the written language of a country like China again bears some resemblances to the latter's colonial past that should not be underestimated.

While the previous examples have shown that a sense of inferiority can easily be instilled as long as Latin-based scripts seem to be the 'natural' script to be used in conjunction with technologies in general, the process of developing the underlying technological standards adds another level of hierarchy: These are often drafted in and imported from former colonial powers, thus hierarchies extend to notions of cultural superiority and inferiority, because even the inventions made in other parts of the world nevertheless will have to comply with the standards defined in Europe and North America. Neither the Seagate hard disk and the AMD processor manufactured in Malaysia, nor the creation of the Blue-ray disc by a group of companies based largely in East Asia can conceal the fact that generally these products and inventions are expected to seamlessly integrate with the said standards one way or the other.[16] Intellectual property rights further hinder the adaptation of ICT and crucial technologies as well as standards are kept under the auspices of their inventors: The control over the Global Positioning System (GPS), for example, remains firmly in the hands of the United States government, and the Department of Commerce has only given up its influential position within the Internet Corporation for Assigned Names and Numbers (ICANN) in October 2009.[17]

However, once technologies have become out-dated, the low-cost markets become dumping grounds for these technologies, often ignoring the actual requirements of local clients. This is a serious issue in the context of ICT where obsolete technologies can also pose a security risk, not only for the individual user, but also for the larger community. A survey of 1110 encrypted wireless networks in Penang, Malaysia, a country which has had a fair share of technological development shall substantiate this claim: Despite Malaysia's technologically relative advanced status, only 505 (45.5%) of the routers surveyed were using an up-to-date WPA-encrypted network. The remaining 605 (54.5%) were using a WEP-encrypted network which is no longer deemed secure as it can easily be compromised and is therefore hardly in use anymore in countries such as Germany for a couple of years now.[18] Taking into account those WPA-networks which still offer a WEP-compatibility mode, the number increases to 876 (79%). A network that only features weak encryption may rather lull the user in a false sense of security leaving him or her less aware of the possibly serious consequences when outsiders can get access to personal data easily. The reason for the continuous use may be the cheaper cost of these out-dated routers as well as compatibility issues with older hardware used in

---

16 This is not to say that there are no groundbreaking technological developments from outside the European / Northern American region. East Asian companies and consortiums, for example, have on a number of occasions invented technologies or contributed to their development which resulted in standards such as the VHS tape or the DVD. However, the fact remains that in most cases the underlying standards still needs to be adhered to, in this case the PAL/NTSC signal transmission standards.

17 ICANN controls the internet root servers and allocates top-level domains (such as .com or .de). In short, it controls the namespace in the internet. See http://www.icann.org/en/announcements/announcement-30sep09-en.htm.

18 In a similar survey in Germany, only one out of 24 wireless networks was unprotected and one out of six was using the weak WEP encryption, see "WLAN-Netze bisher nicht flächendenkend sicher", http://www.teltarif.de/wlan-sicherheit-bundesgerichtshof-urteil-folgen/news/40964.html.

these networks.[19] These developments add to the uneven playing-field, and although different in their extent, these aspects also resemble the relationship between the colonizers and the colonized societies where the latter were either cheap producers of goods or profitable selling markets.

Conclusion

With the points mentioned in this chapter, I have raised questions regarding the underlying structures of technology, especially ICT. I have argued that ICT do not exist in a neutral environment, but reflect norms, practices and hierarchies of the societies that surround them. This is especially significant for postcolonial societies as it is in this respect that more general perspectives on the impact on ICT show their limitations when structures of power are underestimated, be they in terms of center and periphery or technological considerations that ignore demands and requirements of marginalized societies due to economic power.

However, perceptions that ICT are a means for growth, development and a harbinger of liberal values are often times still central focal points regarding the role and function of ICT, whereas the issues raised in this chapter are rather seldom taken into consideration or even downplayed. Instead of euphemistic idealizations or pessimistic critiques of ICT as a whole, a multifaceted perspective is needed, also when it comes to search for ways to enable and increase participation through the use of ICT in postcolonial societies. It is neither appropriate to demand that everyone should learn English and regard this euphemistically as an additional qualification that enables to participate in the global sphere, nor are approaches of localization always outright beneficial because new boundaries may emerge, as the example of the use and implementation of IDN has shown.

Thus, while the positive effects of ICT should not be ignored, they need to be juxtaposed with the impact they have on people's lives, in order to prevent a

---

19 Routers were surveyed in the Georgetown-Jelutong-Gelugor area of Penang island using automated wireless network monitoring software Barbeloo with subsequent XML evaluation.

creeping reinforcement of unjust hierarchies and one-way flows of knowledge and technologies, glossed over by positive developments for an IT-savvy elite.

While these issues have been addressed in this chapter to a limited degree, a number of questions still need to be addressed and this chapter could only highlight a few. The different levels of influence of technological blueprints have been touched upon in this article, but more fundamental questions are still waiting to be encountered which I would like to group into four pillars: Firstly, there is the methodological framework which is needed to approach the question of measuring the impact of ICT and related developments. Where this has not been done, the hypotheses raised in this article will need to be backed up or falsified by qualitative or quantitative findings. Doing so will be difficult not only due to the necessary development of suitable measuring categories, but also to identify a long-term 'before/after' environment. Due to the far reaching deployment of ICT that has reached almost every corner of this planet and is incorporated into daily life in many areas, this will be a challenging task as a clear distinction of cause and effect may become difficult beyond a level of personal, in-depth interviews. Alternatively, a qualitative inquiry would have to extend the trans-disciplinary approach to socio-psychological disciplines in order to find out in which way a change of perception and behavior has taken place.

Secondly, and connected to this would be questions dealing with the ways and levels in which these developments and impacts reflect a colonizer/colonized dichotomy. As this chapter has shown, it can not be assumed that malevolence towards different languages and cultures was a driving force behind non-inclusive technological designs and blueprints. Nevertheless, the resulting effect may evoke shared images and experiences of a perceived disadvantaged culture, language or development that need to be examined in order to identify clearly the various levels of impact of ICT.

Yet I would not propose to use a term like 'cybercolonialism' to describe these relations. While I would argue that marginalized societies in the Global South bear a heavier burden than otherwise marginalized societies and therefore require the abovementioned multi-layered perspective of analysis, a strict colonizer/colonized dichotomy would underestimate the different impacts within marginalized societies in the Global South. The respective centers in colonized and colonizing countries may have more in common in terms of technological development, use and appropriation than the centers and peripheries in one given country and the same may apply for the peripheries. In addition to that, this would also conceal the significance of the adaptation and transformation of ICT that is also relayed back to other parts of the world as I have shown elsewhere (Holst, 2007). These do take place despite the critical questions raised in this chapter: On the one hand, the use of higher capacity SIM-cards in mobile phones in Southeast Asia is a case in point where a specific approach was taken to increase the usability of these often ill-equipped phones to store larger amounts of SMS messages at a fraction of the cost of a more advanced device. On the other hand, ICT can also provide important means for example to challenge authoritarian rule: The Multimedia Super Corridor (MSC) in Malaysia is an example where a means to tap on foreign ICT expertise led to a digital public sphere largely free from censorship that became a backbone of the rise of the political opposition. The third pillar of research would therefore deal with developments in which adaptation and transformation of ICT have gone unexpected ways and have shown an impact on marginalized societies beyond the colonizer/colonized dichotomy.

Deriving from that is the fourth pillar of research questions, centered on the issue of how postcolonial societies react to this development. While the clear economic imbalance and the long established advantage based on habitual experience and knowledge of ICT may lead to a further reinforcement of these relationships, this is by no means certain. Especially nations that had to bear outright sanctions by ICT-leading countries and industries, such as China or countries in the Middle East may opt to go or have already gone their own ways in establishing suitable ICT infrastructure, as Khater (2010) suggests.

A more refined approach is therefore necessary to take into account the specific histories and experiences in marginalized societies. While this may be obvious on a more general perspective, dedicated postcolonial approaches that take up findings from media and communication studies are still far and few in between, although such trans-disciplinary approaches are important to holistically grasp the issues at stake. A joint disciplinary perspective of media-, area- and postcolonial studies that comes with a reciprocal questioning of each others' postulations and findings will thus provide for a foundational critical framework needed to address the issues at stake comprehensively.

Bibliography

ANDERSON, W., 2002. Introduction: Postcolonial Technoscience. *Social Studies of Science*, 32 (5-6), pp. 643-658.

ARTHUR, W. B., 1994. *Increasing Returns and Path Dependence in the Economy*. Ann Arbor: University of Michigan Press.

DAVID, P. A., 1985. Clio and the Economics of QWERTY. *American Economic Review*, 75 (2), pp. 332-337.

FERNÁNDEZ, M., 1999. Postcolonial Media Theory. *Third Text*, 47 (Summer), pp. 11-17.

FOUCAULT, M., 1977. *Discipline and Punish: The Birth of the Prison*. New York: Pantheon.

FRANZKI, H. & AIKINS, J. K., 2010. Postkoloniale Studien und Kritische Sozialwissenschaft. *PROKLA. Zeitschrift für kritische Sozialwissenschaft*, 40 (1), pp. 9-28.

FRIEDMAN, T., 2005. *The World is Flat*. New York: Holtzbrinck Publishers.

GUNZENHÄUSER, R. & HENNINGER, A., et al. 2001. Von Technik zu Kultur und zurück: Berührungspunkte zweier Forschungsprojekte im Kontext der Chemnitzer Forschergruppe. *Chemnitzer Informatik Berichte*, 2001 (1), pp. 5-19.

HEIDEGGER, M. 1977. The Question Concerning Technology. In: W. Lovitt, ed. *The Question Concerning Technology and Other Essays*. New York: Garland Publisher.

HOLST, F. 2007. Adaptation and Transformation: The Internet: An Alternative Challenge to Authoritarianism? A Short Malaysian Case Study. *Gesellschaft und Politik in Südostasien*, 31, pp. 47-53.

KHAN, Z. A. & KAMARUDDIN, S. & BENG, S. C. 2006. Ergonomic Design of a Computer Keyboard Layout for Malay Language. *Asian Journal of Ergonomics*, 7 (1 & 2), pp. 81-100.

KHATER, R. 2010. Digital Protectionism: Preparing for the coming Internet Embargo. *Arab Media and Society*, 2010 (12), [online] Available at: http://www.arabmediasociety.com/index.php?article=766 [Accessed 30 September 2010].

MAHONEY, J. 2000. Path Dependence in Historical Sociology. *Theory and Society*, 29 (4), pp. 507-548.

MOHD, Z. & ABD, R. & MIKAMI, Y. et al. 2005. Multilingual ICT Education: Language Observatory as a Monitoring Instrument. *Conferences in Research an Practice in Information Technology* 46, pp. 53-61.

POSTER, M. 2007. Postcolonial Theory in the Age of Planetary Communications. *Quarterly Review of Film and Video*, 24 (4), pp. 379-393.

SUCHMAN, L. 2002. Practice-Based Designs of Information Systems: Notes from the Hyperdeveloped World. *The Information Society*, 18, pp. 139-144.

ZHAO, S. & BALDAUF, R. B. 2008. *Planning Chinese Characters: Reaction, Evolution or Revolution?* Dordrecht: Springer.

All URLs checked for availability and content on 30 September 2010.

Saskia Schäfer

Expanding the Toolbox: Discourse Analysis and Area Studies[1]

When I arrived in Malaysia in December 2005 to spend an exchange semester as an undergraduate of Southeast Asian Studies and Political Science, I was delighted about the number of English language magazines and newspapers that I was sure would enable me to understand what was going on – and eventually to provide me with sufficient background knowledge to be able to understand the Malay language papers better. In our Area Studies department, we had a focus on history, but I was eager to incorporate my minor subject of Political Science and follow current political issues. I hurried to purchase the newspapers in the morning, as kiosks usually had only two copies of each paper. Reading, however, left me utterly frustrated. There were sentences and pictures, but I did not learn anything from reading them. They seemed hollow and empty and did not make much sense to me. I tried to read them as 'serious' newspapers, but they did not seem serious enough for that. I tried to read them as tabloids – but they were neither glossy nor dingy enough for that. I quickly learned that my idea of newspapers would not fit and gave up reading them. In Malaysia, I learned, you get your information mainly from online newspapers, magazines and blogs, due to the complex censorship of the print media. Over the period of my stay, I learned about current political issues by listening to lecturers' complaints and discussions and by watching and spending time with people. After some months, I returned to buying the print newspapers and was surprised how much more I was able to understand. I had learned how to read between the lines. Still, there was much that I did not quite grasp; it was as if I were lacking the tools to dismantle some of the barriers. Upon my return to my home university in Berlin, I took a class in media analysis, read up on Discourse Analysis and complemented this with

---

1 I would like to thank Vincent Houben for taking the time to discuss the arguments of this article. I also thank Tobias Berger and the editors of this volume for their helpful comments on an earlier version of this article and I am grateful to Samuel Cuff for his critical remarks and the language editing.

courses on modern depictions of 'the Orient' in the department for German literature. I took a fresh look at my own medial and academic environment.

In this article, I will address some of the shortfalls of both Western-centric media studies, and Western-centric social science in general, and show how approaches from both Discourse Analysis and Area Studies can be used to fill in some of the gaps. I argue that thorough background knowledge is necessary in order a) to avoid simply transferring models derived from the specific experiences of modern Western Europe and, connected to this, b) to meaningfully embed media analysis in wider socio-political developments. Such knowledge includes familiarity with the language(s) used, the wider societal context and the historical dimension. Furthermore, as analysing and understanding do not happen in an extra-discursive space, c) the necessity for awareness applies not only to the observed matter and region, but to the research itself. I thus stress the importance of locating the researcher's position within the discursive network. I draw on examples primarily from research conducted in Malaysia, particularly on the debates on apostasy and religious freedom between 2001 and 2007. The role of religion within the post-colonial multi-religious Malaysian society is controversially debated and these debates crystallise in what is often framed as 'religious freedom' or 'apostasy'. The importance of Islam within the political system is reflected in the dual law system: So-called Syariah Courts (Sharia Courts) run parallel to Civil Courts and deal mainly with issues related to family matters of citizens categorised as Muslims. Raising the Syariah Courts to that status is often interpreted as a result of a process usually referred to as 'Islamic revivalism' or 'Islamisation'. In the research I draw from for this chapter, I looked at the dynamics of both legal and medial discourse and found that the dynamics between the two are very revealing when combined with a perspective on government institutions and organisations.

The Impact of Discourse Analysis

Discourse Analysis approaches involve the investigation of discourse phenomena. The academic interest in the relationship between language and political action became prominent in the 1960s, within what later was to be known as structuralism and post-structuralism or, in broader terms, during the developments following the Linguistic Turn (of the first half of the 20th Century). Discourse Analysis approaches are used in a variety of academic disciplines, including linguistics, history, anthropology and political science. Based on notions of power being de-centred and de-personalised (esp. Michel Foucault), it is assumed that power is to a large extent realised through the production of knowledge. While discourse is not the only framework within which, and by use of which, power is exercised, it plays a key role in understanding a society's power relations. As is well known, the theoretical works that provide the basis for Discourse Analysis approaches also provided an important fundament for what is often referred to as 'Post-Colonial' studies. Edward Said, whose publication of 'Orientalism' in 1978 is often seen as a founding work of postcolonial theory, developed his ideas among others on the basis of Foucault's work, particularly on the idea that knowledge and power are inseparable. Said initially aimed his criticism at the academic discipline of 'Orientalism', the study of oriental languages and 'cultures' and the predecessor of today's Area- or Islamic studies. He pointed out the connections between the study of 'the Orient' and its partial colonisation. This criticism has left its highly visible marks in academia, even beyond the classical 'orientalist' disciplines. According to Said, *the Orient* and *the Oriental* were brought into being through their study; they were *discursively created*. 'The Orientals' were represented by someone else, by travellers and scholars from colonising countries; they were said to have been denied their right to self-representation. Employing discourse or media analysis in studying societies outside one's own could be seen as an attempt to take the 'observed object' seriously and give back the right to self-representation: instead of relying solely on one's own observations as a foreign researcher, one places a focus on the various local perspectives.

How are problems identified and dealt with? How is communication structured within the society; who speaks, who does not; what can and what cannot be said? Of course, the researcher herself is always involved in the discourses she analyses. It is crucial to acknowledge this and we will return to this in the section *Situating the Researcher*.

Discourse Analysis and its Various Schools

The approach of Discourse Analysis has developed into several branches. Generally, the objects of such analyses include written, spoken and signed language, as well as – depending on the definition of discourse – other semiotic events. Discourse consists not only in what is said, but also in what is not said or not *say-able*. Different schools have developed different focuses; some are much closer to detailed textual analysis (Jäger, 2004), while others stress the connection between discourse and power (Laclau and Mouffe, 1985). Some of these approaches differentiate between discursive and non-discursive elements and others stress the discursiveness of everything we perceive. There is no overriding consensus about methodology or collective definitions. Definitions of the notion of discourse differ, as well as the ways of relating discourse to institutions and to other concepts such as knowledge, truth and social practice.

A number of text-oriented approaches have been developed, mainly between the 1970s and the 1990s by sociolinguists within the schools of 'Critical Discourse Analysis'. Some examples include the works by Norman Fairclough (1989), Teun van Dijk (1985) and Siegfried Jäger (1993). They demonstrate how texts can be analysed in great detail. They also offer methods and guidelines which train to *read between the lines*. As mentioned above, Discourse Analysis approaches cross disciplinary boundaries. One of their most important strengths is that they allow for analysis at various levels and do not limit research to either a macro- or a micro-perspective. They also do not limit themselves to a meso-level, but offer the possibility to examine the dynamics between the different levels. The understanding of discourse employed in this article is based on approaches of Critical Discourse Analysis. While acknowledging that all elements of a society were at one point discursive, it differentiates between discursive and extra-discursive elements.[2] This differentiation is an analytical tool to facilitate a view at the dynamics between several elements. Some scholars (Bührmann and Schneider, 2008) call this the relationship between discourse and *dispositif*, or apparatus (Michel Foucault)[3]. Such an

---

[2] A discussion of the degree of separation between these is beyond the scope of this article. See Bührmann and Schneider, 2008.

[3] For more on Foucault's concept of the dispositif, see for instance Colin Gordon (1980: 194-228).

understanding seems most adequate here to support the argument that approaches of Discourse Analysis can address the dynamics between elements at the organisational-institutional level, such as a certain law, for instance, and the level of representations and medial debates. I will go into more detail about this point in the section below on discourse and its wider contexts.

Discourse and Media Analysis

Obviously, one significant area of discourse formation is media. As the 'Fourth Estate', a country's media have traditionally been closely associated with the political system. One of their main functions in a liberal democratic system is to be part of a system of checks and balances. Freedom of the press is a mechanism of control that is strongly defended rhetorically. However, this is only one reason for the importance of the media in a political system. What is more important within the context of Discourse Analysis is the fact that media coverage – as any discourse – does not only *reflect* a society's other discourses, institutions and social practices, but also *influences* them. Debates between the candidates become an increasingly observed element of election campaigns, politicians' presence and appearance in the media are widely discussed and, in some cases, media personnel run for positions in government institutions. In the German language, the word '*Mediendemokratie*' (literally: media democracy)[4] illustrates this increasing importance. It is within this context that the discourse plane of media is approached here. Even when focussing solely on a specific discourse in a particular medium, such an analysis will be embedded in its larger context, and usually involves illuminating discourses and the ways in which their representations connect to other levels of society, such as its legal structures and politico-institutional settings. Especially in combination with an examination of other social practices, and in particular the dynamics between them, the analysis of a mediated debate enables the researcher to identify important incidents, actors and strategies. When looking at a society other than one's own, one inevitably draws comparisons to the system one is familiar with. It is very important, however, to keep in mind that different

---

4   The literal English translation is for assistance only. The English term 'media democracy' actually has a different meaning than its German counterpart, which I will not elaborate here.

societies and their media systems emerge/d and develop/ed in divergent ways in different parts of the world.

Troubleshooting: Discourse Analysis and Malaysian Debates

Malaysian society is a case where our tools of analysis have to be altered and the toolbox expanded. Malaysia's population reflects its colonial history on many levels. Several political organisations and parties have remained basically the same since the last years of colonial rule and so have many legal institutions. During the 19th century and the early 20th century, the British brought in workers from China and India to maximise the profits from their resource-rich colony. Additionally, the area of which today's Malaysia is a part lies at the crossroads of earlier trading routes and attracted trading communities from many parts of the world. Today, in addition to the 60% of the population classified as Malay and indigenous, there are Malaysians of Arab, Chinese, Indian, Indonesian, Portuguese and Thai descent, to name only the most prominent groups. Besides Malay and English, several Indian languages and Chinese dialects are widespread and taught in schools, not to mention the several indigenous languages used in the East of the country. The media system reflects this diversity. Several daily newspapers are printed in each of Malay, English, Chinese and Tamil. Radio and television stations are run in the various languages and even the cinematic landscape features not only the common links to Hollywood and Bollywood, but also to the Tamil language film scene in the Southern Indian state of Tamil Nadu.

This multiplicity of languages makes it difficult to directly apply some of the methodologies and guidelines that were developed by scholars of Discourse Analysis, based on the media systems of contemporary Western Europe. Most contemporary Western European countries have a clear majority language dominating the public space. While there are publications in other languages available in most metropolises, such as newspapers in Turkish, Polish or Chinese, these are categorised as 'specialist' and are aimed at rather small language communities, who are generally also fluent in the country's majority language.

Secondly, in addition to *language*, one has to take the different *kinds of media* into account. Access to different kinds of media varies between countries and regions. Literacy rates are high in Malaysia.⁵ If I looked next door to Laos I would face a very different situation, and it would be necessary to find out whether a focus on print media would make sense at all, or whether a study would be better suited to concentrate on a country's radio or television landscape, for which a significantly different set of methods would have to be applied, possibly even developed. Technically the same, a medium can play a very different role in different societies, not always depending on the rates of distribution. The fact that China has extended its digital censorship to sms text messaging services, for instance, suggests that this medium has played a significant role in political discussions. Thus, before jumping to an analysis of a particular medium, it has to be situated within its particular media environment.

As already indicated by the example of the sms text messaging censorship in China, different kinds of direct and indirect *censorship* lead to different techniques of writing and reading between the lines. They also invite the usage of other media. In Malaysia, the complicated censorship mechanisms vary to a large extent between offline and online media. Although freedom of speech and freedom of press are enshrined in Article 10 of the Constitution, the Malaysian media face structural restrictions on two major levels. First and foremost, there are legal restrictions, most importantly the Printing Presses and Publications Act, introduced in 1984⁶ and amended in 1987. This law requires the annual renewal of a publishing licence, which is at the sole discretion of the Ministry of Home Affairs. Newspapers whose journalists have offended the government face the threat of having their licence withdrawn or not having it renewed, while the respective journalists face legal charges. Malaysian journalists have complained about the large variety of laws that can be used to silence critics, for instance the Sedition Act and the Law of Defamation. Thus, many journalists have become accustomed to self-censorship, resulting among other things in widespread cautiousness.⁷

---

5   Unicef estimates a total adult literacy rate of 92%. http://www.unicef.org/infobycountry/malaysia_statistics.html (Accessed 23 September 2010)
6   The act then replaced the Printing Presses Act of 1948 and the Control of Imported Publications Act 1958/1972.
7   Conversation with Jason Tan, editor of the Malaysian magazine 'Off the Edge', 13 March 2010 in Kuala Lumpur.

One consequence of this cautiousness is that online media have developed into a much more commonly drawn on source for critical assessment of what is going on. While social network sites and blogs are often used for entertainment and consumption, they are also an important source of critical journalism, in some societies more than in others. (see Holst in this volume and Jurkiewicz in this volume). While digital media and their impact are very important, the role of print media continues to be significant, especially in dialogue with digital media. This is also due to limited internet access, for instance in rural areas. In some areas, both the internet and print media might play only a secondary role and television might be much more important.

So far, we have seen some of the difficulties that can occur when trying to transfer models of media analysis from contemporary Western Europe to other contexts without adjustment. Of course, there are differences within Western European media systems, for instance regarding ownership issues, lobbying and different ways of dealing with the right to privacy. However, the differences between system parameters are even greater when compared to, for instance, post-colonial semi-authoritarian systems. Examples of potential differences are, as we have seen, the role of language, the role of certain types of media, and restrictions such as direct and indirect censorship and ownership structures.

The difficulty of transferability applies, of course, not only to the sphere of media. As mentioned above, media analyses are always to be seen within their larger context. Of course, the difficulties involved in transferring models are equally pressing here. The following two sections will thus illustrate two arguments: that media observations always have to be connected to other discourses and practices; and that the theoretical assumptions and methodological tools derived from Western European contexts have to be critically evaluated and adjusted.

Embedding Media in the Wider Context

Besides locating the various media within their media environment, it is absolutely crucial to situate them in their wider societal context and to connect observations on the discursive level to other spheres, such as the legal-institutional sphere and that of daily practices.

A look at the coverage in the mainstream daily print newspapers of Kartika Dewi Shukarno, a Malaysian woman who was to become the first woman to be caned under Sharia law in Malaysia for consuming alcohol in 2010, suggests that Malaysian Muslims live in teetotalism. A stroll through Kuala Lumpur's nightlife would reveal that such an assumption is far from reality. It is obvious that large parts of daily practices are simply blanked out in the medial debates. This gives the media coverage a different background to that in Bangladesh, for instance, where drinking is far less common. Additional information is necessary to get a more complete picture of any discursive event, since no action is independent from the discourses surrounding it, and vice versa. Following a notion of power as dispersed and difficult to localise, the mechanisms that are not observable on the surface have to be taken into account. Observations from the medial level have to be embedded in the larger *dispositif* or apparatus, in order to facilitate meaningful conclusions. Important incidents, as for instance legal amendments (of a state or national constitution) might not be covered in the media; either due to censorship or a focus on more current, pressing issues. Media also depend on coincidences and seasons, for instance the 'silly season' might bring up issues that would otherwise have been ignored. In short, the analysis of media discussions without connecting those to insights gained through other methods could result in a distorted picture of events.

Pointing at the diversity in language above has already indicated that other 'cleavages' have to be taken into account when analysing societies one is not familiar with. Often, linked to language is the category of 'ethnicity'. This concept plays an important role in many societies and this is not only reflected on the discursive level, but also in political organisations and institutional structures (if one follows a definition of discourse that separates between the two). Language and ethnicity are only two examples of such categorisations, others that play a different role than in contemporary Western Europe could be the role of age, gender, family ties or clan structures.

Thus, it is hardly surprising that the difficulties that emerge during the transfer of analytical categories to other discursive settings equally occur when trying to transfer such models to analyses of the political in general.

In Malaysia, a citizen's ethnicity ('*bangsa*' or 'race') is usually noted on the birth certificate and can play a decisive role in the distribution of employment and access to education. The political party system is to a degree based on 'race' affiliations. Parties of the governing coalition include the United Malays National Organisation, the Malaysian Chinese Association and the Malaysian Indian Congress. This characteristic is not unique. Many post-colonial states have inherited or developed structures that emphasise other political affiliations than the European class-based system from left to right. Other possible fundaments for parties are regional ties, as in some systems in francophone sub-Saharan African countries, and parties based on, and repetitively referring to, religion, as for instance in Israel, Turkey and India. Researchers coming from Western-centric political science often simply locate religious parties such as Indonesia's Partai Keadilan Sejahtera (PKS), which is often compared to the Muslim Brotherhood in Egypt, at the conservative end of a political spectrum, based on Western Europe's historical context. This ignores those forces within the party that represent a modern and fresh alternative to the government and the fact that many vote for them because of their takes on corruption, their promises to stand in for the interests of the less wealthy, and the party's young and enthusiastic members. While Malaysia's Islamist party Parti Islam SeMalaysia (PAS) campaigns against corruption and patronage politics as well as organising free health care tours in rural areas and promoting human rights, they also demand Sharia law and in 2001 showed their solidarity with Afghanistan's Taliban. Prima facie, some of their actions would have them classified as 'leftist' and 'progressive'/'liberal', while other characteristics of these parties could be categorised as conservative or 'right wing'. These examples show that the political schemata derived from very specific historical circumstances are insufficient to fully grasp other contexts. Thus, new perspectives have to be developed in order to understand the dynamics between different groups in societies.

The political constellations I have described here, differing from the right-to-left-spectrum, are both reflected in and shaped by a society's media system. It is therefore crucial to interpret a society's media discourses based on detailed knowledge of its recent history and wider context. An advantage of Discourse Analysis approaches is their multi- and interdisciplinarity. While it is of course often essential to conduct detailed research on certain aspects of a society, a simultaneous look at several analytical layers, such as what is usually classified as micro- and macro-levels, is necessary in order to understand larger developments. An analyst of political and legal institutions who is not aware of a society's wider political discourse will have difficulties in interpreting the sudden emergence of certain institutions. Often, institutions emerge and legal changes occur that would be surprising without background knowledge of the public debate preceding them. Knowing the debate is crucial in coming to understand major institutional and organisational changes. An example for this is the quasi ban of the Ahmadiyah, an Islamic religious movement, in Indonesia in 2008.[8] The ban of their *dakwah* activities by the secular government came as a surprise for those who focussed entirely on institutions. It came after constant lobbying and protest by Muslim groups usually categorised as extremist, such as the Front Pembela Islam (FPI). Notwithstanding the fact that these groups enjoy little support among the general public, critics argue that their demands for further Islamisation and their campaigning against the Ahmadiya finally resulted in the ban. In this case, it was clearly the public discourse that pushed forward a certain agenda and caused its translation into a policy. And again, it is necessary to understand public discourse to see that the ban does not have full support by the majority of the citizens. A mere look at the legal or political level would not suffice here. Knowing the discourse surrounding such institutional changes helps to understand and analyse them meaningfully. To be able to estimate the impact of legal changes it is important to know what certain lobbyists have actually aimed at/been campaigning for and what resistance had been formulated. Who were those lobbyists and what role did they play? Parts of these wider contexts can be exposed through media analysis.

A perspective on media can help to identify some important actors that would otherwise probably have been neglected. An example of this is the role of religious authorities, which would be, from a Western-centric starting point, underestimated, if taken into account at all. Coming from a Western-centric political science perspective, the actors commonly taken into account are political parties. Even though concepts of civil society have filled in the analytical gap between the governmental and institutional level and the individual,

---

8   On 9 June 2008, the Indonesian government declared a joint ministerial decree ‚freezing' activities of the Ahmadiyah community. This compromise allowed Ahmadiyah members to practice their faith, as long as they would not do not try to disseminate it to anyone else.

even here the role of religious organisations and authorities is often underestimated or misinterpreted. For instance, regulations and fatwas[9] issued by religious authorities may be seen as a 'traditional' and 'backward' way of dealing with problems, but might actually be a recent development in the society, or one that has only recently gained popularity and importance, and thus represent a very modern phenomenon.

To give an example of a potential misinterpretation or simplification: The fact that the categories 'Malay' and 'Muslim' are connected on both the legal and the discursive level in Malaysia[10] should not hide the fact that there are also many Muslims of Indian and Chinese origin. The underrepresentation of these non-Malay Muslims in medial and daily discourse is not a coincidence but a political mechanism, and can be explored through a careful analysis of this specific discourse within its larger context. In this particular example, the simplifying representation of Muslims as Malays – which is more clearly observable in media which are more directly influenced by the government – supports the divisive politics of the ruling coalition along ethnicised lines, and is interlinked with policies such as the quota systems for *bumiputeras*. The precondition for such an analysis is of course knowledge of other factors within that society, in this case Malaysia.

This knowledge concerns not only a society's major historical events and narratives, as well as developments of its politico-legal system, but also the basic level of language. The subtleties, innuendos and indirect references of a text cannot be grasped without some knowledge of a language's heritage in form of narratives, stories, books, and films. Traditionally, a large part of Area Studies consists in learning the language thoroughly. This is usually done through language courses, but also through the discussion of literature, film and other forms of traditional and contemporary art, which offer access to societal issues. It is generally common to spend longer periods in the region and some universities encourage such stays through co-operations for intensive language courses, home stay, or exchange programs. The process of understanding the layers of a society is deepened through *active participation*

---

9   A fatwa is a religious opinion concerning Islamic law, usually issued by an Islamic scholar.
10 A Malay is constitutionally (Art.160) defined as someone who speaks the Malay language, practices Malay custom and confesses to the religion of Islam.

rather than only *passive observation*. Texts are perceived differently once one has not only read in the language, but also written in it; one observes dances differently when one has been taught the steps, and understands the importance of certain foods better once having participated in preparing them. Knowledge acquired through such active participation can facilitate the interpretation and understanding of private and micro-level discussions as well as public debates. Some allusions might be the crucial part of an article, but would otherwise seem pointless or be passed over unnoticed. One line might turn the whole meaning around. The same is valid for cultural performances and political gatherings, where what is being said can be contradicted or emphasised by a certain dress or the employment of certain cultural devices.

Historical Dimension

An example for the necessity to embed a discursive event within a larger debate was the waiving of the *keris*[11] by the then UMNO Youth Chief Hishamudin Hussein in 2006 and the media coverage of this event. The traditional Malay weapon was unsheathed and waived during an assembly of UMNO's youth wing. One cannot possibly understand the meaning of this without some background knowledge about this signifier. The *keris* was originally used before the arrival of Islam in the region (ca. 13th century) and was connected to the courts in the Hindu-Buddhist era. Later, most probably during the colonial period, it was transformed into a marker of ethno-nationalism (Noor, 2009). It is placed at the centre of the UMNO's flag and is connected to the infamous riots in May 1969, which are usually referred to as 'race riots'. Another often cited discursive event is a rally held by UMNO youth in 1987, where Najib Tun Razak, who later became Prime Minister, is accused of having threatened to 'bathe the *keris* with Chinese blood.'[12] This discursive history of the *keris* makes up the background against which this recent event has to be interpreted. Hishamudin later apologised, but many observers criticised his actions and

---

11 The *keris* or *kris* is an assymetrical dagger and considered both a weapon and a spiritual object in the wider Malay world.
12 Retrieved from: http://www.limkitsiang.com/archive/2000/dec00/lks0596.htm (Accessed 4 October 2010)

belated apology and blamed these as the main reason for the ruling coalition's poor performance at the elections.[13]

Understanding the complexity of political symbolism requires in-depth knowledge of historical trajectories, politico-cultural developments, and linguistic subtleties. The example also illustrates how a perspective toward discursive events can combine looking at both the organisational framework that constitutes production of discourses as well as the factors influencing their reception.

The importance of an historical dimension to such analyses is obvious – no tracing of a discussion can be fruitful without a look at its development. One does not have to be a follower of path dependency or slip into simplistic divides along 'cultural' lines to acknowledge the importance of historical background for contemporary developments. A major problem is the disparity with regard to background knowledge of different societies. While a course on contemporary political developments – wherever it is taught – will assume (implicit) knowledge of major historical events in European history, references to 'other' societies will always have to be lined with extra information about historical events. The importance of references to history is not always obvious because much of the knowledge is internalised and is implicitly recalled. For concrete studies, there are of course reasons to conduct synchronic analyses, for instance for comparative reasons. But in order to connect such analyses to more general conclusions about a society, it is necessary for the researcher to be aware of its wider historical development, even if this background knowledge is not made explicit.

Interdisciplinarity and Area Studies

Taking the wider context into account lies at the heart of both Area Studies and Discourse Analysis. Both approaches acknowledge the potential of a multi- and interdisciplinary perspective on society and emphasise how problematic monocausal explanations can be. Sticking to the example of the role of religion in Malaysia, instead of tracing the developments usually called

---

13 Hisham's 'keris' apology: Your say, 28.04.2008; http://malaysiakini.com/news/82020; (Accessed 7 September 2010).

'Islamisation' or 'revivalism of Islam' only back to the influence of *dakwah*[14]-groups within a worldwide 'revival of religion', of which Malaysia is no exception, such an approach could consider the rivalry for constituencies between the two Malay-Muslim based parties UMNO and PAS and the interlinked harsh criticism aimed at what Malaysia's former Prime Minister Mahathir framed as 'the West'. The combination of these approaches allows a simultaneous look at the institutional and organisational level as well as the level of representation and that of daily interaction. Such combinations of macro-and micro-analysis offer great potential for the understanding of broader developments, especially if they are systematically connected to more detailed and focussed studies of singular phenomena.

The Researcher's Dialogue with the Region

As has already become clear, the researcher herself is of course at no point located 'outside' the discourses. She will always perceive the observed discourses through the screen of her own world view and interpret the object of research within her *horizon*. Employing Hans-Georg Gadamer's notion of horizon[15] (1960) here emphasises the potential of the alleged outsider's limitations. Horizon is to be understood as enabling interpretation through the limitations: On the one side the horizon limits the view, but on the other side these limitations make it possible to view the subject-matter in relations to others, to put it into perspective. In other words, it is not possible in the first place to understand anything but from one's own horizon. Going further, a researcher's horizon (of experience or tradition) is as much part of the process of understanding/interpreting (*Verstehen*) as the counterpart's horizon (of meaning); this is encapsulated in Gadamer's notion of a fusion of horizons (*Horizontverschmelzung*), which at the same time acknowledges and transcends particularities (Gadamer, 1960). Using this notion for Area Studies, the aim cannot be an objective outsider's account of a distanced and fixed subject-

---

14 'Dakwah' is the Islamic invitation to Islam, usually aimed at fellow Muslims.
15 I am well aware of the complicated theoretical relationship between approaches of hermeneutics and (post-) structuralist and (de-)constructivist approaches. Only a handful of publications deal explicitly with the different histories of reception between the works of Gadamer and Foucault (Kögler, 1999; Vasilache, 2003). In this article, I do not intend to go deeper into that relationship, but only utilise the concept of ‚horizon' to emphasise my argument.

matter, but rather the fluid and flexible interpretation of a society's events and developments. Our understanding of such things flows and shifts as it is interpreted and re-interpreted by various people at various times. The process of understanding cannot be limited to measuring something and integrating it into existing thought patterns, or adding new insights into the way we see ourselves and the world around us. Surpassing mere appropriation, encountering new and 'other' horizons will have to effectively change this worldview, our horizon. The basic assumption here is that one meets new experiences with the fundamental awareness that *the Other could be right*.

One particular contribution of Area Studies here is the detailed knowledge and long-term relationship of the researcher with the region, ideally including longer stays. As described in the examples above, the researcher's anticipations and worldview are likely to be questioned and challenged when encountering and trying to grasp a society other than her own. Of course, such an encounter can also and does often have the opposite effect: prejudices always carry the potential of being 'confirmed' by an actual experience. But such an encounter, and in particular a long-term engagement that involves travelling back and forth between different regions, does offer the potential to challenge and alter someone's worldview, possibly even fundamentally. With such an altered perspective, a further encounter with a region – both a foreign one and one's 'own'– will again be commenced from a different starting point. The unfamiliar is made familiar and the familiar is made unfamiliar. Instead of one epistemological rupture or break, this is rather to be understood as a constant dialogue that includes such ruptures and changes of perspective. Thus, the process of researching and understanding/explaining will have to be conducted on at least these two levels: Observing and *interpreting the subject-matter* while at the same time acknowledging and excavating *one's own pre-judgements*. This is similar to locating the researcher as a discourse participant within the larger *dispositif* or apparatus in which discourses operate.

Situating the Researcher

Taking the theoretical assumptions behind Discourse Analysis seriously, a researcher will document and lay open her own assumptions to the largest extent possible (at least to herself), as part of the process. This would include documenting the expectations and identifying the underlying hypotheses. Field notes and keeping a research diary can both support such identification during the early phases and serve as a basis to discover tacit knowledge when referred to at a later stage. Self-observation is a key part of ethnographic work and there is no reason not to transfer this to a media analysis, even when conducted from afar. Field notes and research journals differ from other forms of academic writing and are thus much more suitable for tracing and discovering hidden assumptions. They are not written in order to be presented and are thus closer to one's immediate thoughts. Notes, as opposed to research papers and reports, record ruptures and turbulences as they happen, rather than portraying the process in a linear way. Such turbulences might be personal and subjective, or much more connected to the actual subject-matter, but the strength of the research journal is precisely that this artificial separation is not necessary; all the different aspects that constitute a research project are free to mingle and melt together. Some suggest supplementing written research notes with photographs; the increasing tendency to audio- (and even video-) record interviews in addition to taking notes could be seen in relation to this.

Important parts of my research are the research questions that drive me. Having written down those questions every couple of months during the first phase of my current research, it is interesting to look back and compare them. Looking at them reveals a great deal about my own assumptions and situates me within the larger discursive net within which I explore other discourses and their interconnectedness. The great difficulty herewith – which, although it is the topic of many academic debates, I can only mention here[16] – lies in finding a balance between a vain search for a fictive objective truth and 'hard data' on one hand, and a paralysing, over-relativising self-exploration that does not allow for any comparisons and generalisations on the other.

---

16 One such debate is that between the advantages and weaknesses of quantitative and qualitative methods; and on a more abstract level there are questions about the existence of truth and objectivity as well as universality versus particularity.

Conclusion

This article has attempted to exemplify some of the difficulties that arise when attempting to transfer models of analysis based on the specific context of modern Western Europe to other regions. This applies to the sphere of media, but more generally to any analysis of socio-political phenomena and developments. These difficulties do not mean that we have to reject theoretical and methodological approaches derived from specific empirical contexts. The crucial point is, however, that the consequence of acknowledging the particularity of these contexts must be to scrutinise them very carefully and to adjust them before applying them to other contexts. To make the unfamiliar familiar, we cannot simply take the shortcut and just pretend its familiarity. Rather, ways have to be developed to make the unfamiliarity fruitful.

One way to meaningfully evaluate such theories and methodologies, as we have seen, is the connection of the media sphere to other discourses and to other elements in a society, such as the institutional and organisational level as well as social practices. Such an embedding of media in their wider context is necessary in any case, but even more so if the connections would otherwise be implicitly modelled upon the very theories and methods we have identified as particular and thus insufficient. Thus, it is crucial to acquire knowledge about the region in question and in doing so meaningfully embed observations from the media sphere into its regional context, in order to be able to draw more general conclusions about socio-political developments.

Precisely here lies also the strength of the interdisciplinary approaches of both Discourse Analysis and Area Studies: Both reject monocausal explanations and open the perspective to the dynamics between several elements of a society. Such dynamics might differ from those observed in contemporary Western Europe. Thus, as argued above, understanding/interpreting/analysing such dynamics in an unfamiliar region requires the simultaneous observation of the matter and the identification of one's own prejudices. This process, I suggested, can among others be facilitated by the use of a research journal. It requires constant self-reflection and continuous fine-tuning and reworking of approaches and categories.

A criticism aimed at Area Studies (sometimes from within) has been the lack of findings and conclusions that are universally applicable. Following the assumption that the dialogical and dialectic processes described earlier carry the potential of constant cross-fertilisation, it is only consistent to strive to make findings from a particular region accessible and usable for other regions. This is reflected in some academic trends to work comparatively over long distances on the basis of structural instead of 'cultural' similarities. It also finds resonance in the tendency to dissolve particularities such as 'Indonesian Studies' and even 'Southeast Asian Studies' into much broader 'Asian Studies'. This holds great potential. However, it is crucial to face the danger of abandoning the interest in the particular for superficiality(involved in the construction of new 'container' concepts), and to meet it with a skilful balance of detail. Discourse Analysis approaches offer tools for such an embedding of the particular into the larger context, especially through facilitating a joint perspective at both the macro- and the micro-level and their mutual influences and connections. Together with thorough knowledge about the area, the combination of two multi-disciplinary approaches that both acknowledge the importance of an interest in very detailed accounts as well as broader analyses, the possible insights hold great potential beyond the areas in question. They could result in not only producing important knowledge about that very region, but facilitating dialogic exchange between particularities and, in a next step, inspiring fresh perspectives on those regions that are usually not perceived as 'particular' or 'regional' – Western Europe, for instance.

Bibliography

BÜHRMANN, A. D. & SCHNEIDER, W., 2008. *Vom Diskurs zum Dispositiv: Eine Einführung in die Dispositivanalyse.* Bielefeld: Transcript.
VAN DIJK, T. A., 1985. *Handbook of Discourse Analysis.* London: Academic Press Inc.
FAIRCLOUGH, N., 1989. *Language and Power.* London: Pearson Education Limited.
FOUCAULT, M., 1984. *Histoire de la sexualité, vol. 3. Le souci de soi,* Paris: Gallimard.
GADAMER, H. G., 1960. *Wahrheit und Methode.* Tübingen: Mohr (Siebeck).
GORDON, C., 1980: *Power/Knowledge Selected Interviews and Other Writings.* London: Vintage Books.
JÄGER, S., 2004. *Kritische Diskursanalyse: Eine Einführung,* 4. Aufl., Münster: Unrast Verlag.
KÖGLER, H. H., 1999. *The Power of Dialogue: Critical Hermeneutics after Gadamer and Foucault.* Cambridge: MIT Press.
LACLAU, E. & MOUFFE, C., 1985. *Hegemony and Socialist Strategy.* London and New York: Verso Books.
NOOR, F. A., 2009. *What your Teacher Didn't Tell You. The Annexe Lectures, Vol 1.* Kuala Lumpur: Matahari Books.
VASILACHE, A., 2003. *Interkulturelles Verstehen nach Gadamer und Foucault.* Frankfurt am Main: Campus Verlag.

List of Contributors

BETTINA GRÄF studied Islamic Studies, Arabic Studies and Political Science in Berlin. She wrote her PhD dissertation on media fatwas with Yusuf al-Qaradawi's fatwas as an example. Currently she is working as a post-doc fellow at Zentrum Moderner Orient in Berlin on the concept of Islam as a political order at the beginning of the Cold War.

FREDERIK HOLST studied communication studies, political sciences and psychology in Penang and Berlin where he also obtained his PhD in Southeast Asian studies. Influenced by scholars of critical psychology, his overall research interest lies in the impact of technology on society. He published on the role of ICT in authoritarian systems and in processes of ethnicization as part of his PhD. His pre-academic work experience as an IT programmer comes in handy at times for his research.

SARAH JURKIEWICZ studied European Anthropology, Islamic Studies and Theatre Studies in Berlin. After her graduation, she worked at Zentrum Moderner Orient in Berlin as assistant to the director. Since 2009 she is a PhD fellow at Oslo University where she is working on blogging in Lebanon from a media anthropology perspective.

MARCUS MICHAELSEN is a PhD candidate at the Department of Media Studies at the University of Erfurt preparing a thesis on the Internet in Iran's political transformation. He received his M.A. in Middle Eastern Studies from the Université de Provence in 2003. From 2004 to 2006 he was a research fellow at the Institut français de Recherche en Iran (IFRI) in Tehran. His research interests include: Media in development and democratisation, Iranian politics.

CLAUDIA NEF SALUZ is a PhD candidate in Social Anthropology and fellow of the interdisciplinary University Research Priority Program Asia and Europe of Zurich University. Her research focus has been primarily on Islam in Indonesia, especially on expressions of piety in every day life among the urban youth. She is the editor of the book "Dynamics of Islamic Student Activism", Yogyakarta: Resist Book, 2009.

CAROLA RICHTER was a lecturer and research associate for International Communication Studies at the University of Erfurt from 2004 to 2010. She received an M.A. in Arabic studies, journalism and political sciences from the University of Leipzig. In 2010 she finished her PhD thesis on media strategies of the Muslim Brothers in Egypt. Her research focuses on Arab media systems and political communication in the Muslim world.

SASKIA LOUISE SCHAEFER studied Southeast Asian Studies, Political Science and Literature at Humboldt University Berlin, spending at least two months a year in the region. In her MA thesis she conducted a detailed media analysis of a Malaysian daily newspaper. She is currently a PhD student at the Berlin Graduate School Muslim Cultures and Societies, focussing on the public debates on religious freedom in Indonesia and Malaysia.

NADJA-CHRISTINA SCHNEIDER is a Junior Professor for Mediality and Intermediality in Asian and African Societies at Humboldt University Berlin. She has a background in South Asian and Islamic Studies as well as in Modern History. Her areas of interest include media developments in South Asia (and beyond), medialization processes and social change, new forms of mediated interaction, and debates about Islam and gender.

FRITZI-MARIE TITZMANN studied South Asian Studies at Humboldt University and Religious Studies at Freie Universität Berlin. Since November 2009 she is pursuing a doctoral degree from the Cross-Section for Mediality and Intermediality in Asian and African Societies of Humboldt University. Her Ph.D. research project focuses on "Local and translocal dynamics of a global media phenomenon: Changing female agency and subjectivity in the Indian online matrimonial market".

INTERNATIONALE UND INTERKULTURELLE KOMMUNIKATION

Herausgegeben von Prof. Dr. Kai Hafez, Universität Erfurt und
Jun.-Prof. Dr. Carola Richter, Freie Universität Berlin

Band 1 Denise Busch: Das Bild Griechenlands zwischen Fremd- und Selbstwahrnehmung. Eine Untersuchung der deutschen und griechischen Presseberichterstattung über die Vorbereitung für die Olympischen Spiele 2004 in Athen. 204 Seiten.
ISBN 978-386596-039-9

Band 2 Sylvia Breckl: Auslandsberichterstattung im deutschen Fernsehen. Die Dritte Welt in Weltspiegel und auslandsjournal. 214 Seiten.
ISBN 978-386596-025-2

Band 3 Christoph Hantel: Journalistenausbildung in Mosambik.
428 Seiten. ISBN 978-3-86596-056-6

Band 4 Karin Keding/Anika Struppert: Ethno-Comedy im deutschen Fernsehen. Inhaltsanalyse und Rezipientenbefragung zu „Was guckst du?!". 208 Seiten. ISBN 978-3-86596-084-9

Band 5 Martin Ritter: Medien und Demokratisierung in Kambodscha.
406 Seiten. ISBN 978-3-86596-178-5

Band 6 Julia Hahn, Larissa Haida, Kathrin Mok, Sheila Kusuma, Michaela Schmid, Kerstin Schulz, Nicolas Schwendemann, Michael Szep: Europa als Gegenstand politischer Kommunikation. Eine Fallstudie zur deutschen EU-Ratspräsidentschaft.
226 Seiten. ISBN 978-3-86596-186-0

Band 7 Lukas Peuckmann: "One World – One Dream"? Das Bild Chinas in der Olympia-Berichterstattung.
260 Seiten. ISBN 978-3-86596-311-6

Frank & Timme

INTERNATIONALE UND INTERKULTUREL KOMMUNIKATION

Band 8   Nadja-Christina Schneider/Bettina Gräf (eds.): Social Dynamics 2.0: Researching Change in Times of Media Convergence. Case Studies from the Middle East and Asia. 170 Seiten. ISBN 978-3-86596-322-2

Band 9   Patricia Carolina Saucedo Añez: Lateinamerikanische Medien in Deutschland. Medienkonsum und -produktion von Migranten. 210 Seiten. ISBN 978-3-7329-0024-4

Band 10   Fritzi-Marie Titzmann: Der indische Online-Heiratsmarkt. Medienpraktiken und Frauenbilder im Wandel. 340 Seiten. ISBN 978-3-7329-0011-4

Band 11   Regina Cazzamatta: Brasilien-Berichterstattung in der deutschen Presse. 254 Seiten. ISBN 978-3-7329-0069-5

Band 12   Danny Schmidt: Das Bild Russlands in den deutschen Leitmedien. Die Berichterstattung über Russland und Wladimir Putin im Rahmen der Ukrainekrise. 172 Seiten. ISBN 978-3-7329-0204-0

T Frank & Timme